IMAGES OF ENGLAND

HULL'S
TRANSPORT

IMAGES OF ENGLAND

HULL'S TRANSPORT

PHILIP C. MILES

TEMPUS

Above left: Hull Corporation No. 103. (RKH 103) a 1954 Coronation class trolleybus is seen on the 63 service to Beverley Road, Queen Victoria Square is in the background.

Above right: Sentinel No. 243, reg. V803 belonging to the Hull Corporation Highways Department.

In loving memory of my dear mother

Frontispiece: The Danish SV *Cap Nord* at Hull, *c.* 1920.

First published 2007

Tempus Publishing Limited
The Mill, Brimscombe Port,
Stroud, Gloucestershire, GL5 2QG
www.tempus-publishing.com

© Philip C. Miles, 2007

The right of Philip C. Miles to be identified as the Author
of this work has been asserted in accordance with the
Copyrights, Designs and Patents Act 1988.

British Library Cataloguing in Publication Data.
A catalogue record for this book is available from the British Library.

ISBN 978 0 7524 4206 6

Typesetting and origination by Tempus Publishing Limited.
Printed in Great Britain.

Contents

Acknowledgements

I would like to thank the following people for allowing me to use their photographs in this book, James Smith, the late Robert F. Mack, W.J. Haynes, Sky Photos, Martijn Nobel, Breyne Photos, Herbart Ballard, Bev Bar photographs, C.W. Routh and also P&O Ferries.

My thanks to Hull City Council libraries (local history section) for their help and information, also thanks to Bryan Fish.

Riverside Quay, Hull, *c.* 1925.

Introduction

The City of Kingston-upon-Hull lies on the northern side of the River Humber and is separated down the middle by the River Hull (from where we obtain our name). Hull is a city steeped in history. The town of Hull was developed over 700 years ago by King Edward I and the old town was once fortified, with the town secure and protected within the old walls. There was always a need to cross both the River Hull and the River Humber. Small ferries, which were little more than open boats, transported people between both banks of the River Hull before the first bridge was built in 1541. Many small boats went across the River Humber to Lincolnshire carrying both passengers and goods, and thus the long tradition of crossing the River Humber began. Over the years many vessels have been used for the ferry service between Hull and New Holland, and this long tradition of ferries crossing the River Humber only ended on 24 June 1981.

As the city outside the town walls grew with the suburbs sprawling ever further outwards, the need for people to travel into the town centre grew accordingly, firstly horse-drawn wagonettes and horse-buses were used to satisfy the public's needs while, in 1875, the first tram system commenced, using horses to pull the trams.

Electric trams entered service in July 1899. The tram system continued to grow as Hull expanded further and further outside the old town and the trams continued to serve the city until the last service operated on 30 June 1945.

Buses began operating in Hull in the early 1900s with City of Hull Tramways operating its first bus service in 1909, and although this service from North bridge and Stoneferry Green was short-lived (lasting a mere three years), this was a form of transport that would provide the kind of strength and reliability that could satisfy both company and customer. With much-improved buses City of Hull Tramways re-commenced bus operation in 1921 with a service between Bond Street and Stoneferry Green, and in 1926 East Yorkshire Motor Services was formed as a result of an agreement between two long-established bus operators in the area, Lee & Beaulah Ltd and Hull & District Motor Services Ltd, to further consolidate the regions services. The buses have gone through many changes in the last hundred years, from the primitive early buses used by City of Hull Tramways to the modern buses of today. Another type of transport used in Hull was the trolleybus and the first trolleybus service began in 1937 and lasted until 1964.

The ferries, trams and trolleybuses are now no more than memories and have passed into the history books. It is hoped that this book will bring back memories of the transport once operated in Hull and, for those who do not remember them, a glimpse into Hull's transport history.

The need to cross the River Hull continues to this day although many of the old bridges crossing the river have been replaced over the years. Nevertheless, it is still interesting to see the bridges which span the River Hull.

Hull continued to grow in the nineteenth-century and its communication links were further improved with the arrival of the railways that would have such a big effect on Britain's landscape. With the many docks scattered along the River Humber the railways were the perfect vehicle to carry freight to and from these highly important trade routes, thus a large rail network was constructed to serve the area.

Much of the railway track was built on embankments above the roads while many of the bridges were constructed to carry the railways over the roads, in fact, many of these still exist today in one form or another. In the docks swing-bridges were constructed to carry the railway lines over the locks and docks and, while many of the old docks are now closed, some of the old swing railway bridges remain.

Another ferry service to be operated from the Port of Hull was, and still is, North Sea Ferries, which now operates as P&O Ferries. This company's inaugural ferry service between Hull and Rotterdam left the Humber on 17 December 1965. Two specially built vessels, the *Norwave* and the *Norwind*, were used to operate the route. Further new ships have entered service over the last forty years and one of the ships (the *Norland*) even saw active duty during the Falklands campaign.

I have tried to capture many of the old bridges, road transport and ferries with a selection of old and new photographs which I am sure will be interesting to both young and old alike, and also to the many people who are enthusiasts in one or more of the subjects covered in this book.

Philip C. Miles
Kingston-upon-Hull

one

The Humber
Ferries

It is known that a ferry service was operated in the Roman times, with some form of ferry operating between Winteringham and Brough. By the twelfth century ferry services ran from Barton to Brough, Barton to Hessle and between North Ferriby and South Ferriby while in 1316 a service began operating between Hull and Barton when Edward II granted a charter. It was used by Royal passengers travelling north to York as this was the most direct route from Lincoln. This crossing was established for many years as the main Humber crossing.

In 1803 a new ferry service began, started-up by a Mr Tommy Dent, who operated from a narrow inlet (or creek) and used the passage from New Holland to Hull for the purpose of smuggling goods across the Humber, this was the start of the long-established ferry service from Hull to New Holland.

The Hull to New Holland ferry service began in 1826 when the PS *Magna Charta I* began operating the service, this was in competition with the Barton ferry service which was operated by the PS *Royal Charter*. Also in operation in 1831 was the 'peoples opposition boat', or the PS *Public Opinion*, (formerly the *Victory*). In 1836 the mail coach from London began using the New Holland to Hull service rather than the Barton route, and then in 1845 the Great Grimsby & Sheffield Junction Railway (later to become part of the London & North Eastern Railway (LNER)) took control of the ferries. The Barton ferry found it was struggling in the newly competitive environment, and in 1851 the Barton to Hull ferry service ceased to operate. The Hull to New Holland ferry service later passed to British Rail.

On 26 June 1914 the paddle steamer PS *Killingholme* was used to officially open King George Dock.

In this form the Humber Ferry so increased the number of passengers using this service that over the years a very large selection of ferries have operated between Hull and New Holland to satisfy demand.

In 1934 the first two of the three magnificent *Castle*-class ferries entered service. These were the PS *Wingfield Castle* and the PS *Tattershall Castle* built by Wm Gray of Hartlepool. They were both launched on 24 September 1934 and indeed were both 199.9ft long. A third *Castle*-class ferry, the PS *Lincoln Castle* entered service in 1940, built by A.&J. Inglis of Pointhouse, Glasgow, she was 209ft long and could carry 914 passengers as well as motorcars.

In January 1948, the PS *Tattershall Castle* was the first paddle steamer ever to be fitted with radar at a cost of £3,000, thus allowing the ferry to cross the Humber in thick fog. The radar proved itself so successful that it was later fitted to the *Wingfield* and the *Lincoln Castle*.

A new means of travel to cross the Humber came in February 1968 when two hovercraft were purchased for a service between Hull and Grimsby. These were the *Minerva* and the *Mercury* and they managed to cut an hour off the ferry's time. However, this service was short-lived, lasting only eight months and it was eventually withdrawn on 21 October 1968.

Both crafts suffered many propeller and shaft breakages during their service. The last ferry to be acquired was the DEPV *Farringford* which was transferred from the Isle of Wight service in 1974. The Humber Ferries continued on for a short while but their days were numbered, and the death knell finally came in 1981 when the Humber Bridge was opened and allowed passage for vehicles across its impressive span. The last day of service by the Humber ferry came on 24 June 1981 and was operated by DEPV *Farringford*.

Over the years there have been other ferry crossings. In 1814 the paddle sloop PS *Caledonia* operated a service between Hull and Gainsborough, whilst in 1815, paddle steamers PS *Humber*, PS *British Queen*, PS *Albion*, PS *Waterloo* and the PS *Maria* worked on the Humber. In 1832 ferry services were operated between Hull and Grimsby, Selby, Thorne, Goole, Gainsborough, Brigg and York. In 1835 the PS *Sovereign* operated between Hull and Selby.

Following these developments a Barton to Hessle service was operated in 1841 by the PS *Ann Scarborough*, whilst a service between Hull and Lindsey was operated in 1843 by the PS *Columbine*. The Gainsborough Steam Packet Co. operated using the PS *Atlanta* for a service between Gainsborough and Hull and also on the routes between Hull, Burton upon Stather, Ferriby and Grimsby.

The PS *Manchester II* was used for services between Hull, Burton upon Stather, Ferriby and Grimsby in 1855 as was the PS *Sheffield II*. The Gainsborough Steam Packet Co. operated the PS *Isle of Axholme* on their service between Gainsborough and Hull in 1860. The PS *Lady Elizabeth* operated a service by the Goole Steam Packet Co. between Hull and Goole in 1890. In 1912 the Goole Steam Packet Co. purchased the PS *Isle of Axholme* to operate this service.

The Hull & Goole Steam Packet Co. operated a service between Hull and South Ferriby using the PS *Her Majesty*, while another paddle vessel that the Goole Steam Packet Co. operated was the PS *Empress* for their Hull to Goole service in 1893. At the time the PS *Humber* was being used on several services up and down the Humber.

Ferries Which Have Operated Between Hull and New Holland

Name	Built By	Year Operated	Year Withdrawn	Remarks
PS *Magna Charta* (I)	–	1826	–	Started the ferry service
PS *Falcon*	–	1845	–	(a)
PS *Prince of Wales*	–	–	–	Purchased from Gravesend Steam Packet Co. in 1848
PS *Queen*	Dichburn & Mare	1842	–	Purchased from Gravesend Steam Packet Co. in 1848
PS *Manchester I*	–	May 1849	1855	–
PS *Manchester I*	–	–	–	Ex-Clyde Steamer given the same name, later renamed *Old Manchester*
PS *Sheffield I*	–	Running in 1849	1855	–
PS *Petrel*	–	–	–	Worked the service in 1850. Hired from the Watermans Co.
PS *Royal Albion*	–	Running in 1860	–	General purpose tug-boat and used as a stand-in ferry
PS *Liverpool*	M. Samuelson of Hull	1864	1899	–
PS *Doncaster*	M. Samuelson of Hull	1864	1899	–
PS *Manchester II*	–	–	Ran aground and broke her back in 1875	Used as a stand-in ferry
PS *Grimsby II*	Earle's Shipbuilding & Engineering Co. Ltd, Hull	1888	1922	Went for breaking-up in 1923
PS *Cleethorpes*	Gourley Bros Ltd	1903	1934	(b)
PS *Brocklesby*	Earle's Shipbuilding & Engineering Co. Ltd, Hull	1912	1935	(c)
PS *Killingholme*	Earle's Shipbuilding & Engineering Co. Ltd, Hull	1912	1945	(d)
PS *Frodingham*	A & J Inglis, Glasgow, built 1895	Operated the service from 1928	1936	Bought by NER Com she was originally called the *Dandy Dinmont*
PS *Wingfield Castle*	Wm Gray of Hartlepool	1934	1974	–
PS *Tattershall Castle*	Wm Gray of Hartlepool	1934	1972	First ever paddle ship to be equipped with radar in 1948
PS *Lincoln Castle*	A&J Inglis of Glasgow	1940	1978	–
DEPV *Farringford*	–	Built in 1947, operated the service from 1974	1981	–

Additional Notes:
(a) Acquired by the New Holland Ferry Co. in 1849.
(b) During the First World War this vessel became a seaplane tender ship, it was later sold to the Redcliffe Shipping Co.
(c) This vessel was used as a seaplane tender ship during the First World War and was later sold for further service on the Firth of Forth and renamed the *Highland Queen*. In 1936 she was sold for scrapping in Germany.
(d) The PS *Killingholme* was used to officially open the King George Dock on 26 June 1914. She was used as a seaplane tender ship during the First World War and during the Second World War was used as a seaplane carrier.

A busy scene at the Hull Corporation Pier *c.* 1900. The PS *Isle of Axholme* is seen alongside the loading stage. This ferry was operated by the Gainsborough Steam Packet Co. and operated between Hull and Gainsborough. In 1912 the Goole Steam Packet Co. purchased the PS *Isle of Axholme* for their service between Hull and Goole. Also visible alongside the PS *Isle of Axholme* is the tug *Tollman*. In the centre of the photograph is the old frigate ship, HMS *Southampton* which was converted into a training ship for poor boys from broken homes. On the right is HMS *Galatea*.

The PS *Manchester* is seen at the landing stage at Corporation Pier, (Victoria Pier) whilst other small boats are also visible on the river.

The PS *Brocklesby* saw twenty-three years of regular service between Hull and New Holland. She then gave further service on the Firth of Forth, where she was renamed the *Highland Queen* before going for scrapping in Germany in 1936.

Built by the local shipbuilders of Earle's Shipbuilding & Engineering Co. Ltd, the PS *Brocklesby* was originally constructed in 1912. She was owned by the Great Central Railway and then the London & North Eastern Railway. The PS *Brocklesby* became a seaplane tender vessel during the First World War and operated the ferry service between Hull and New Holland from 1912 until 1935.

The PS *Cleethorpes* was built by Gourley Bros Ltd. She was 190.1ft long and operated the ferry service between Hull and New Holland from 1903 until 1934. During the First World War the PS *Cleethorpes* was used as a seaplane tender vessel. She was later sold to the Redcliffe Shipping Co.

Seen here at Corporation Pier is the PS *Doncaster*, this ship was built at Earle's Shipbuilding & Engineering Co. in Hull in 1888. The PS *Doncaster* was owned by the Manchester, Sheffield & Lincolnshire Railway, she was the second vessel to carry this name and was the first steel-built ship for this railway company. She operated the Hull to New Holland service between 1888 and 1922, but after 1912 her status was lowered to being that of merely a stand-in vessel. She was withdrawn in 1922 and scrapped in 1923.

Built in 1934 the PS *Tattershall Castle* was one of three sister ships, the *Tattertshall*, the *Wingfield Castle* and the *Lincoln Castle*. Built by William Gray & Co. of Hartlepool for the London & North Eastern Railway, she was launched on 24 September 1934 by the daughter of Sir Murrough Wilson (chairman of the LNER), Miss Pamela Wilson. Used during the Second World War to ferry troops she was withdrawn in 1972 when she became a floating art gallery on the Thames. In 1981 she was sold again and in 1982 became a bar on the Thames.

In 1934 two new paddle steamers entered service on the Hull to New Holland Service. These were the PS *Wingfield Castle* and the PS *Tattershall Castle*, built by William Gray of Hartlepool. Both vessels were launched on 24 September 1934. Seen in her later British Rail livery is the PS *Wingfield Castle*, which was withdrawn from service in 1974.

Sister ship to the *Wingfield Castle* is the *Tattershall Castle*, these paddle steamers could carry 1,050 passengers as well as a small amount of vehicles. The PS *Tattershall Castle* was the first paddle steamer to be fitted with radar. In 1940 a third *Castle* was added to the fleet, the *Lincoln Castle*.

The PS *Lincoln Castle,* the last of the three *Castle* paddle steamers, will always be remembered by many Hull people. Seen here departing from Corporation Pier in her smart British Rail livery on the hour-long journey to New Holland, the PS *Lincoln Castle* was built by A.&J. Inglis of Glasgow. She operated the ferry service between 1940 and 1978, giving thirty-eight years of regular service.

The PS *Lincoln Castle* was the last paddle steamer to be made for the Hull to New Holland service, she was built in 1940. She could carry 914 passengers and twenty cars. Operated by the London & North Eastern Railway, and later British Railways, the PS *Lincoln Castle* was the last coal-burning steamer operating in Britain. Seen in her last years in service and in her final livery of white and black with red and black funnel, she is seen here approaching the Hull Corporation Pier.

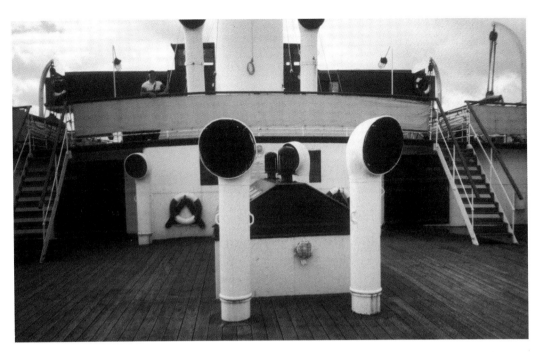

The PS *Wingfield Castle* was withdrawn in 1974, sold several times and was eventually left lying derelict in Swansea bay. Purchased by Hartlepool Borough Council she returned to Hartlepool in 1986. This photograph shows the *Wingfield Castle* back at Hartlepool moored on the site of her builder's shipyard. The wide decks of the paddle steamers can be seen in this photograph looking towards the bow and the bridge.

In 1974, a second-hand ferry arrived for the ferry service. This was the *D.E.R.V. Farringford*. Built in 1947 for the Isle of Wight ferry service. The *Farringford* was a large vessel and could carry 796 passengers and forty cars. The *D.E.R.V. Farringford* operated the last ferry service between Hull and New Holland on 24 June 1981.

Corporation Pier

A ferry boat Dock Act in 1801 led Hull Corporation to construct a pier which was parallel to the shore to accommodate the Humber Ferry. In 1847 it was joined to the mainland by a platform. By the mid-1880s it had been altered again and included an upper and lower promenade along with a floating pontoon. It was last rebuilt in the 1930s. Although many people refer to it as Victoria Pier, its correct name is Corporation Pier. Queen Victoria however, did use the pier in 1854.

A number of paddle steamers can be seen in this view at the Corporation Pier in Hull *c*.1910. Just behind the pier is the entrance to Humber Dock basin.

Opposite above: In February 1968 a new service using hovercraft was introduced, this was operated by the Humber Hovercraft Services Ltd. The service operated between Hull Corporation Pier and Grimsby docks. The service used two hovercrafts and the *Minerva* is seen here.

Opposite below The other hovercraft used was named *Mercury*. The service was short-lived due to the high cost of hovercraft maintenance. Both craft suffered many propeller and shaft breakages and the service was withdrawn on 21 October 1968.

Looking west on the River Humber estuary and Corporation Pier. This is where the ferries for New Holland sailed from. The pier was altered several times and this *c.*1909 postcard shows the rebuilt pier with its upper and lower promenade (built in 1882). On sunny Sundays, ladies in their long dresses and sun umbrellas and gentlemen in their Sunday best and bower hats would enjoy a stroll along the Pier.

A busy scene at Corporation Pier, also known as Victoria Pier. In this undated photograph a boat is seen entering the Humber Dock basin, whilst a cargo boat is seen at the Pier. On the right is the Minerva public house.

The old landing stage at Hull Corporation Pier. From here you once caught the ferry across the Humber to New Holland where a train would be waiting for you to take you onto Cleethorpes. The ferries are now just a memory.

At one time the old pier on a sunny Sunday would have seen hundreds of people coming for a stroll to watch the ferries arrive and depart. Few people now venture to this area. The Deep is just visible behind the pier.

A Walk from Hull Corporation Pier to North Bridge

We start our walk at the Hull Corporation Pier, where we look across the River Humber towards Lincolnshire, here the ferries used to set sail for New Holland. We walk down Nelson Street heading east and turn at the mouth of the River Hull. On our right can be seen the Deep, the Worlds only submarium. As we continue walking up-river we see the remains of the old Central dry dock and also the remains of the old South bridge. We carry on, passing the Millennium walk bridge, which, if we decide to walk over, leads us to the Deep. Straight in front of us is the Hull tidal barrier which was opened in 1980 and to date has been lowered 250 times, a process which has saved the old town from flooding on many occasions. From here we can now see Myton bridge carrying the main A63 trunk road.

We carry on walking north up-river towards Drypool bridge, and we see the remains on the right of the old Crown dry-dock, whilst on our left the old warehouses are now luxury apartments. As Drypool bridge comes nearer we pass William Wilberforce's house and the trawler *Arctic Corsair*. After a few minutes we reach Drypool bridge. Here we go onto the bridge and cross over the road to the opposite side of the River Hull. This is known as the Garrison side. As we continue to walk on the right-hand side of the river we pass the old Union Dry-dock on our right and another old dry-dock is visible on our left. A little further on our left can be seen the old entrance to the old Queens Dock, this is the Queens Dock basin. We are only allowed to walk a little further to North bridge and this is where we turn around and retrace our steps back to Drypool bridge. We cross the bridge again and this time walk on the right side of the River Hull, passing Clarence flour mills which opened in 1952, replacing an earlier mill destroyed during the Second World War. We pass the old Drypool basin on our left, at one time a pumping station stood here. We carry on passing underneath Myton bridge and, heading south, we come to the Millennium walk bridge. We walk across the walk bridge back to the west side of the river, again passing the old Central dry-dock, back onto Nelson Street and towards the pier. Finishing our walk from Hull Corporation Pier to North bridge, as we walk up the River Hull we can just wonder how busy the River Hull was in years gone by with its numerous dry docks and the many ships which would have gone up and down the River Hull discharging cargo.

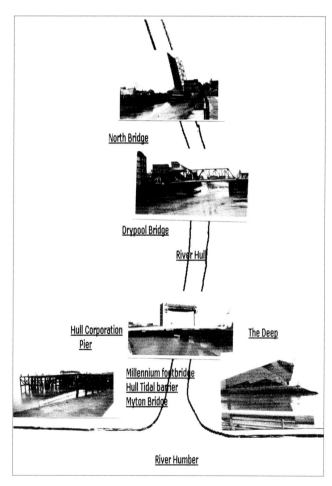

North Bridge

Drypool Bridge

River Hull

Hull Corporation Pier

The Deep

Millennium footbridge
Hull Tidal barrier
Myton Bridge

River Humber

two

North Sea Ferries

NORWAVE

North Sea Ferries came into being with the growth of the motorways in Europe and the British mainland. More and more freight was being transported by road in the 1960s, a trend that continues to this day. Major ports on the Continent were linked by major motor routes which led to containerization, with unit loads becoming more and more popular. Road freight was rapidly taking over from rail freight.

Mr Ian Churcher, a leading figure in European transport circles, saw the desire from all parts of the UK, especially the Midlands, the north of England and Scotland, for freight to be transported between England and the Continent and vice versa, as consumer culture took an increasing hold. As a result, a consortium of six European interests, consisting of two British, two German and two Dutch companies, invested in a programme of two specially built, drive-on drive-off vessels. Not only were they to be designed for carrying freight but also for private cars and foot passengers.

So, the dawn of the North Sea Ferries age had come, and the dream became a reality when the two ships specially designed for this purpose entered service. On 17 December 1965 the first of these vessels, the *Norwave*, set off on her maiden voyage. She could carry 249 passengers as well as cars, trailers and freight. Her sister ship, *Norwind*, built to the same specifications, duly entered service on 22 March 1966. From this date it was possible to operate six days a week. The service between Hull and Rotterdam (Europoort) proved immediately popular both with freight and foot passengers and operations were soon expanded to seven days a week.

Growth of the service continued and in the 1970s two much larger vessels entered service on this route, primarily because of increased capacity in both freight and passengers (particularly necessary in summer). To help out with the freight carried or projected to be carried, North Sea Ferries chartered a number of ro-ro freighters and two lift-on lift-off vessels.

Two brand new vessels were ordered and these were much larger and could carry more passengers and much more freight. The new vessels were built at A.G. Weser in West Germany, the same yard which had built the earlier two vessels. The new ships were named *Norland* and *Norstar*. These huge ships could carry 1,243 passengers, a large increase on the other two ships' 249 passengers, with an enormous cargo area. The first of the two sister ships, the *Norland*, made her maiden voyage on the night of 10 June 1974, followed by the *Norstar* which entered service in December 1974.

The freight-only service between Hull and Zeebrugge soon became the new route for the *Norwave* and the *Norwind*, and both these ships operated on this route from 1974 until 1987, when they were replaced by the *Norland* and the *Norstar*.

The service between Hull and Zeebrugge was now able to carry passengers as well for the first time and this route soon became popular with foot passengers as well as freight.

In 1981 North Sea Ferries became a joint venture between the P&O Group and the Netherlands company Royal Nedlloyd Group, with both companies having a 50 per cent share in the operation. Both companies owned two vessels each, *Norwave* and *Norland* were owned by the P&O Group and the *Norwind* and *Norstar* by the Royal Nedlloyd Group.

In April 1982 the unforeseen happened: Argentina invaded the Falkland Islands. As the Falkland Islands flies the British flag, the government deployed a Royal Navy Task Force to the South Atlantic. The Ministry of Defence requisitioned many British-registered merchant vessels to support the warships. The *Norland* was one of them. After her journey from Rotterdam on the morning of 17 April she discharged her cargo and passengers and was then moved from her berth to No. 7 quay at King George Dock. The *Norland* was quickly converted into a troopship and also had two Sea King helicopter decks fitted, one aft and the other amidships. By 21 April the *Norland* was ready to play her part with the Task Force.

Captain Don Ellerby sailed her down the Humber and into the North Sea heading for Portsmouth, carrying sixty volunteers. At Portsmouth 900 personnel from the Paratroop Regiment's 2nd Battalion embarked on the *Norland* ready for the long journey south. On 26 April the *Norland* set sail for the Falkland Islands. It would be nine and a half months before she would return to Hull.

North Sea Ferries brought in contingency plans for passengers booked to travel on the *Norland* on 17 April, and so some passengers were transferred on to the Hull to Zeebrugge route, or indeed were transferred to other ports. To cover for the *Norland*, North Sea Ferries chartered the passenger vessel *Viking 6*. It was whilst with North Sea Ferries that *Viking 6* carried HRH the Duke of Edinburgh on 9 August 1982. *Viking 6* was replaced in November 1982 by the *Saint Patrick II* which was chartered between November 1982 and April 1983.

In January 1983, the *Norland* was released and then her new orders were for her to return home. The *Norland* was due to have a large homecoming welcome on 1 February, but with winds gusting to hurricane force together with a rapidly ebbing tide the 90mph winds made the docking of the *Norland* impossible, so it was decided to sail once more to sea. In the early evening the *Norland* made her journey up the Humber and into the Port of Hull. Many hundreds of people gathered at the quayside to welcome her and the crew safely home. After a few days, the *Norland* made the short trip to Immigration Graving Dock where she was de-militarised and fully refurbished in a multi-million pound refit. She returned to her normal route on 20 April 1983.

In 1986 two new vessels were under construction as part of an £80,000,000 investment programme. The *Norsea*, which represented P&O's 50 per cent share in the deal, was built in the Govan Shipbuilders yard at Glasgow, whilst the joint partners in North Sea Ferries, Royal Nedlloyd, was building its sister ship, the *Norsun*, in Japan by Nippon Kokan K.K. On 9 September 1986, at the Govan Shipyard, *Norsea* was named and launched by HRH Queen Elizabeth the Queen Mother. The *Norsea* arrived in Hull on 4 May 1987. Four days later she made her maiden voyage on the Hull to Rotterdam route. The *Norsun* arrived in Amsterdam on 5 May 1987 carrying 800 Nissan cars. She entered service out of Europoort on 12 May.

In January 1987 a decision was made to lengthen both the *Norland* and the *Norstar* by inserting a 20.25m mid-section, increasing their cargo capacity by 30 per cent. The contract for the work went to Bremerhaven Yard of Seebeckwerft AG, the original builders of these two vessels. With the arrival of the two new vessels in May 1987, the *Norland* and the *Norstar* sailed to Germany for work to be done, taking seven weeks to complete. Upon completion they were painted in the new North Sea Ferries livery of blue and white. Both vessels started operating the Hull to Zeebrugge route early in July 1987.

The *Norwave* and *Norwind* were sold to the Ventouris Group of Greece and renamed *Italia Express* and *Grecian Express* respectively. Sadly, neither vessel saw much service with their new owners, as the *Norwave* suffered a serious explosion during rebuilding in 1988 and was a total constructive loss. The *Norland* became a total constructive loss after its sinking in 1993.

Since 1996 P&O North Sea Ferries has been a subsidiary of the P&O Ferry division. In 2002 the *Norsea* and *Norsun* went through a £7,000,000 refurbishment: the old cabins were replaced with new cabins, the economy cabins and reclining seats were replaced with new cabins, while the buffet restaurants were renovated, each now with an *a la carte* restaurant and wine bar.

The two new super ferries, the *Pride of Hull* and the *Pride of Rotterdam*, now operate on the Hull to Rotterdam route. The *Norsea* and *Norsun* were transferred to the Hull to Zeebrugge route. The two new super luxury cruiseferries were built at the Fincantieri, Marghera Yard in Venice, each vessel costing £90,000,000. These new vessels must be the ultimate in ferries

– and the largest in the world, they are capable of carrying 1,360 passengers on each vessel along with 250 cars and 400 lorries and trailers. They have a crew of 141. The new vessels are like floating five-star hotels. Inside, the vessels have a bureau de change, a cyber café, shops, children's area as well as an Irish bar, two cinemas, a casino and a show lounge where evening entertainment is shown. Each vessel has 546 cabins, which not only include standard cabins built to a high standard but also fourteen luxury cabins, four staterooms and two suites.

On 27 April 2001, the *Pride of Rotterdam* was officially named by HRH Queen Beatrix of the Netherlands. She began her regular sailings between Hull and Rotterdam on 1 May 2001. Her sister ship, the *Pride of Hull* was officially named in Hull on 30 November 2001 by Cherie Blair and entered service on 2 December 2001.

The first ships to be purchased by the newly formed North Sea Ferries were the *Norwave* and the *Norwind*. The *Norwave* is seen in her original black, white and orange livery with no fleetname. Built by A.G. Weser in Bremerhaven, West Germany, she entered service on 17 December 1965 for the route between Hull and Rotterdam.

A PICTORIAL HISTORY OF NORTH SEA FERRIES

NAME OF VESSEL	BUILT	BUILDER	WITHDRAWN	REMARKS
NORWAVE	DEC 1965	A.G. Weser, Bremerhaven, West Germany	1987	
NORWIND	March 1966	A.G. Weser, Bremerhaven, West Germany	1987	
NORLAND	June 1974	A.G. Weser, Bremerhaven, West Germany	2002	Chartered by the M.O.D. in 1982
NORSTAR	Dec 1974	A.G. Weser, Bremerhaven, West Germany	2002	
NORSUN	May 1987	Nippon, Kokan K.K. Yokohama, Japan		Renamed Pride of Bruges in 2003
NORSEA	May 1987	Govan Shipbuilders. Glasgow		Renamed Pride of York in 2003
PRIDE OF HULL	Dec 2001	Fincantieri, Marghera Yard. Venice		
PRIDE OF ROTTERDAM	May 2001	Fincantieri, Marghera Yard. Venice		

CHARTERED PASSENGER FERRY SHIPS

Name of vessel	Chartered from	Chartered to	Remarks
VIKING 6	April 1982	November 1982	To cover for the Norland
SAINT PATRICKII	November 1982	April 1983	To cover for the Norland

The *Norwave* is seen at the opening of the new lock at Zeebrugge in July 1985. The *Norwave* was registered in Hull and therefore flew the British flag. She could carry 249 passengers. The *Norwave* operated the Hull to Rotterdam service from December 1965 until June 1974 before going on to the Hull to Zeebrugge route from June 1974 until June 1987.

The sister ship of the *Norwave* was the *Norwind*. Registered in Rotterdam she flew the Dutch flag. The service speed of both vessels was sixteen knots.

The *Norstar* dressed overall is seen at Hull, with the Royal Yatch *Britannia* on the left. H.M. the Queen was visiting Hull on 13 July 1977 whilst doing a coastal cruise around Britain to commemorate Her Silver Jubilee.

The *Norstar* is here seen in the later livery of white and blue with large blue fleetname. This vessel, like its sister ship the *Norland*, was built by A.G. Weser of Bremerhaven, West Germany. She was much bigger than the previous two vessels with an original passenger capacity of 1,243. She is seen here after a 20.25 metre mid-section had been inserted.

The *Norstar* is seen in the livery of its new owner P&O Ferries. The livery was later modified. The *Norstar* is seen here at Zeebrugge in May 1997. She operated this route from 6 July 1987 until she was withdrawn from P&O service in 2001.

The sister ship of the *Norstar* was the *Norland*. The *Norland* operated the Hull to Rotterdam route from June 1974 until it was requisitioned by the M.O.D. in April 1982, returning to regular service in April 1983. It is photographed here in 1974 when still new.

A superb birds-eye view of two of North Sea Ferries vessels crossing the North Sea. On the left is the *Norwave* operating the Hull to Zeebrugge route whilst the much bigger *Norland*, operating on the Hull to Rotterdam route, overtakes the *Norwave*.

North Sea Ferries took delivery of two brand new vessels in 1987, these beautiful vessels were named *Norsea* and the *Norsun*. The *Norsea*, seen here, was built by Govan Shipbuilders of Glasgow. Registered in Hull, she flies the British flag. She operated the Hull to Rotterdam route, displacing the established *Norland* and the *Norstar*. The *Norsea* is seen after arrival at Hull, new from the shipbuilder's yard.

The *Norsea* could carry 1,250 passengers. The interior of this magnificent vessel was as good as a five-star hotel. The *Norsea* is seen departing from Hull on her maiden voyage on 8 May 1987.

The sister ship to the *Norsea* is the *Norsun*, registered in Rotterdam she flies the Dutch flag. The *Norsun* was built by Nippon Kokan K.K. of Yokohama, Japan. At the time they were built, the *Norsea* and *Norsun* were the largest ships of their type ever ordered for service from the United Kingdom. After leaving Japan the *Norsun* carried 800 Nissan cars to Amsterdam.

The interiors of the *Norsea* and the *Norsun* are like the inside of a five-star hotel. This view shows the Moonlight lounge.

In 2003 the *Norsea* and the *Norsun* were renamed *Pride of York* and *Pride of Bruges* respectively. The *Norsun* is seen in her new P&O livery

The ultimate in ferries are the two largest flagships to enter service with P&O Ferries. The *Pride of Rotterdam* and the *Pride of Hull*. These new ships are the largest and most luxurious ferries to be operated, costing £90,000,000 each. The shipbuilders were Fincantieri, Venice,

The sister ship to the *Pride of Rotterdam* is the *Pride of Hull*. Both vessels operate on the ten-hour crossing between Hull and Rotterdam. These two vessels are the largest cruise ferries in the world. The *Pride of Hull* was officially named by Mrs Cherie Blair in Hull on 30 November 2001 with the ceremony taking place inside the ship. Both vessels have a maximum speed of 22 knots.

North Sea Ferries also operated freight-only ferries. The *Norbank* and its sister vessel, the *Norbay*, were built in 1993 by Van der Giessen-De Noord of Holland. The *Norbank* is photographed here in the smart blue and white livery.

Whilst the M.V. *Norland* was in the South Atlantic during the Falklands campaign, North Sea Ferries had to charter vessels to cover her. M.V. *Viking 6* was one vessel chartered to cover the *Norland*. It is the only ship operated by North Sea Ferries to have ever carried royal passengers, when H.R.H the Duke of Edinburgh sailed to Rotterdam from Hull on 9 August 1982.

The *Norland* is seen here in her original black, white and orange livery. She is photographed at her berth in Hull on a winter's night ready for the long overnight sailing.

Important Dates for the *Norland*

Year built	1974
Maiden Voyage	10 June 1974
Requistioned by the MOD as a troopship in the Falkland campaign	17 April 1982
Served with the Task Force	April 1982–January 1983
Returned back to Hull	1 February 1983
Sailed once more on the North Sea Ferries route to Rotterdam	20 April 1983
Went for major lengthening	May 1987
Started operating the Hull to Zeebrugge route	July 1987
Final service, arrived at Zeebrugge	28 February 2002

The *Norland* 1974-2002 – Special Feature

Built by A.G. Weser, of Bremerhaven, West Germany and completed in June 1974, the *Norland* was put onto the Hull-Rotterdam service with her maiden voyage from Hull on 10 June 1974. She and her sister ship, *Norstar*, were, at that time, the largest ferries of their kind in the world. She was 153m ((502ft) long, with a capacity of 1,243 passengers along with 500 cars or 134 x 12m units and seventy-two cars. She had two Stork/Werkpoor-type TM410 engines totalling 18,000hp and a crew of ninety-nine. The *Norland* was registered in Hull and therefore flew the British Flag.

From June 1974 until April 1982 she worked the route between Hull and Rotterdam on her regular overnight crossing, carrying thousands of passengers in the process. Passengers on the overnight crossing could enjoy the crossing in style in luxurious lounges, the dance floor and even a casino.

However, the steady crossing between Hull and Rotterdam was about to change. The *Norland* was requisitioned by the Ministry of Defence to carry troops to the Falklands as, in view of the serious international tension at the time, the Government had decided to send a Royal Navy task force to the area. After its return trip from Rotterdam on 17 April 1982 she discharged her passengers and cargo. She was then moved to No. 7 quay at King George Dock, where she was converted into a troopship. On 21 April, under the careful eye of Captain Don Ellerby and sixty volunteers, the *Norland*, which had already taken on some troops, sailed down the Humber to the North Sea. The journey took her south to Portsmouth where last-minute preparations were made to the vessel and further troops of the Paratroop Regiment's 2nd Battalion joined the ship. Also, two Sea King helicopter decks were erected on the vessel. On 26 April she left Portsmouth for the long journey to the Falkland Islands. On 23 May, HMS *Antelope* was sunk and the *Norland* sailed with the survivors of HMS *Antelope*.

For many months the *Norland* stayed in the South Atlantic. Even after the campaign had finished she remained in use and worked the route between Port Stanley and Ascension Island, carrying troops and civilians along with stores and equipment.

By the end of 1982 it was decided that she should come back home. The *Norland* made her long journey back to the east coast and arrived back in Hull on 1 February 1983. After her return she went to Immingham Graving Dock, where over the next eleven weeks she was de-militarised and had a multi-million refurbishment. She returned to her normal duties on 20 April 1983.

Four years after she had returned home, a decision was made to lengthen her and the *Norstar*. In May 1987 she and the *Norstar* went back to their original builders, by now renamed Bremerhaven yard of Seebeckwerft AG. At the builder's yard she was cut into two and a 20.25m section was inserted between the two halves. At the same time improvements were made to her interior. In the new length she would be able to carry 900 passengers with more space for cargo. She was moved onto the Hull to Zeebrugge service in July, carrying a smart new blue and white livery.

She continued on this service until February 2002 when she made her last journey from Hull on the night of 27 February. In 2002 she was sold to SNAV and was re-named SNAV *Sicila* for a service between Naples and Palermo.

Above: Off to war: a rare photograph of three North Sea Ferries docked at Hull in this April 1982 photograph. The *Norland* seen on the left is pictured preparing for her long voyage to the South Atlantic. In the centre is its sister ship *Norstar* with the *Norwave* seen on the right. It would be many months before the *Norland* would once again sail from the Port of Hull

Left: The *Norland* returns. After many months serving in the South Atlantic and being used as a troop-carrying vessel, the *Norland* finally returned to Hull. She is seen here arriving home on 1 February 1983. Strong winds prevented her from entering the Humber during the day and so she arrived back in the late evening.

Opposite above: Eleven weeks after the *Norland* had returned back to Hull and was fully refurbished in a multi-million refit she returned to service. She is seen here back in her original condition in May 1983. A Kingstonian Leyland Leopard with Plaxton Supreme bodywork is seen in the foreground, Kingstonian was owned by Kingston upon Hull City Transport.

In 1987 the *Norland* was literally cut in half when it was decided to lengthen the vessel. The vessel went to the original builders and was then cut into two halves and a mid section measuring 20.25 metres inserted. Compare this photograph with the other photographs of the *Norland*. She was painted in the new blue and white livery with a large blue North Sea Ferries fleetname.

In this February 1998 photograph at Hull the *Norland* is seen in P&O Ferries livery. On the left is the *Norsun*.

Arriving at Zeebrugge for the last time, 28 February 2002. Cheerleaders with P&O coloured flags welcome her in.

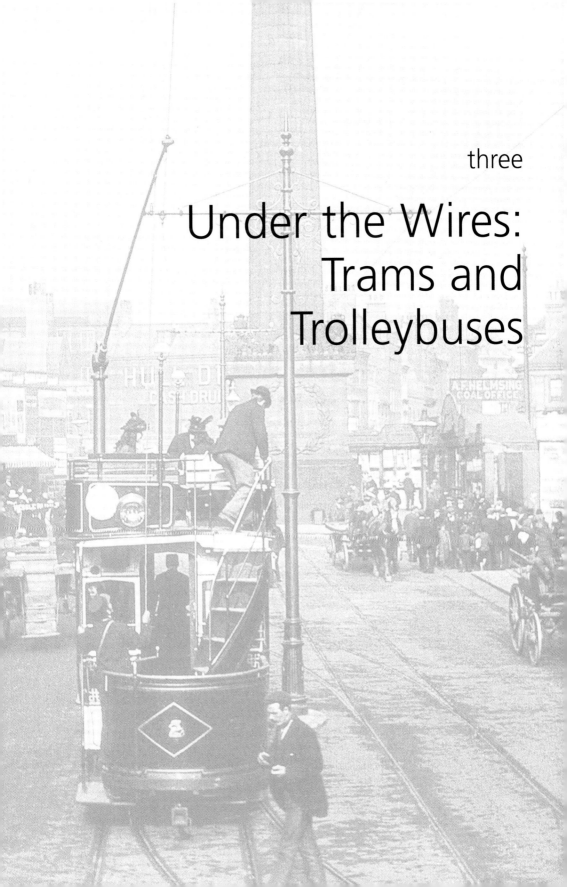

three

Under the Wires: Trams and Trolleybuses

On 9 January 1875, horse-drawn trams first appeared on the streets of Hull, the operators were formed by a London Syndicate and traded as the Hull Street Tramways Co. They operated a service from Savile Street to Beverley Road, but they in turn were owned and operated by the Continental Tramways Co. until they were handed over to the Hull Street Tramways Co. on 1 November 1876.

New horse tram routes soon opened-up as demand increased. On 12 December 1876, a service between Prospect Street and Spring Bank began, while on 7 April 1877 the service from Osbourne Street to Hessle Road started, with others operating to Holderness Road, Hull Pier via Whitefriagate and Anlaby Road by 9 August 1877. In total, nine miles of mainly single-line tramways were constructed with passing loops.

Both single and double-deck trams were operated. The double-deck horse trams were open-top and could seat between thirty-two and forty-four passengers. They were pulled by two horses, with the exception of the service to Spring Bank which was operated by only one. The single-deck horse trams could only seat sixteen passengers and their limited capacity had a bad effect on the company's performance. Indeed, due to the increased competition from wagonettes and horse buses, the company was eventually wound up.

In 1885 the Corporation purchased the horse tramway for the sum of £12,500 and started operating services on 1 August 1896. Times were moving on though and inevitably the horse tramway came to an end on 30 September 1899. By then the steam tramway was well established, having started operations on 21 May 1889, operated and owned by the Drypool & Marfleet Steam Tramway Co., operating a service between Great Union Street and Hedon Road to Lee Smith Street. This was one of the last steam tramways to be opened in the UK and it consisted of seven enclosed steam locomotives and eight fully enclosed trailers with seating for seventy-two passengers. The steam trams could reach a maximum speed of 8mph which dropped to 4mph through the points. In 1899 the system was purchased by the Hull Corporation and then leased back to the company. On 13 January 1901, the last steam tram operated in the streets of Hull.

The first electric tram began operating in Hull on 5 July 1899 under the banner of the City of Hull Tramways, the company eventually came to operate between St John Street and Hessle Road and between St John Street and Anlaby Road. The cars were basic with open roofs and no cover over the stairs, whilst the motorman was open to the elements. They were also limited in their capacity with the early trams capable of carrying only fifty-one passengers.

Nevertheless, the electric tram system continued to grow and new services soon opened up to other parts of the city, including Holderness Road on 10 April 1900, followed by Spring Bank, Beverley Road, the Pier, Hedon Road, and Spring Bank West with several extensions to the original routes. The last extension of the tramway system came on 3 January 1927, when service SW was extended along Chanterlands Avenue north to Cottingham Road as route SWC.

Newer cars entered the fleet in 1905 and these had fixed roofs, although the stairs remained open and the motorman still had no protection against the weather. In fact it was not until 1915 that improvements to the trams were made. A vestibule was fitted which protected the motorman from bad weather, the balcony and stairs were also covered whilst the front of the balcony was extended to the front and rear of the tram to form an open canopy. Development continued and the first fully enclosed cars entered service in June 1920.

The City of Hull Tramways had an unusual way of displaying which route the tram was operating; large boards were used on the front and rear of the upper deck displaying in large letters:

A:	ANLABY ROAD	AP:	ANLABY ROAD/ PICKERING ROAD	B;	BEVERLEY ROAD
BC:	BEVERLEY ROAD/ COTTINGHAM ROAD	D;	DAIRYCOATES		
DP:	DAIRYCOATES/ PICKERING PARK GATES	H;	HOLDERNESS ROAD		
S:	SPRING BANK	SW;	SPRING BANK WEST/ WALTON STREET		
SWC:	SPRING BANK WEST/ COTTINGHANM ROAD	M;	MARFLEET		
P:	PIER VIA OLD TOWN	TH.	HOLDERNESS ROAD via Drypool Bridge		

On several routes the trams operated on a reserved track in the middle of the road, while over the years the older trams were modernised, top covers were added between 1905 and 1909 and the trams were fully enclosed by 1931 by which time more modern trams were entering the fleet. The last tram to enter service did so in 1925 with the No. 113.

On 5 September 1931 the P service to the Pier was withdrawn and this heralded the start of Hull Tram's slow decline. The last tram route to be operated was the D route to Dairycoates on 30 June 1945.

Hull's Trolleybus System

The idea of operating trolleybuses goes back to 1929 when Hull Corporation Tramways looked at various other trolleybus systems. A route operating trolleybuses in Hull was considered, initially this was to run from Paragon Square to Preston Road via Craven Street and Newbridge Road. However, the idea of running trolleybuses was rejected by the Towns Committee.

In 1936 Hull Corporation Transport were given the necessary Parliamentary powers to operate trolleybuses. It was envisaged that the trolleybus services would replace the trams which, under the 1934 co-ordination agreement between East Yorkshire Motor Services and Hull Corporation Transport, had to be replaced as the trams operated in the 'B' area mainly on reserved track.

The first trolleybuses to enter the fleet were twenty-six Leyland TBs's with Weymann fifty-five-seat bodywork. On 23 July 1937, the trolleybus service was officially opened and the first trolleybus service began on 25 July, service 61 to Chanterlands Avenue.

Over the next eight years, the following routes were added:

Service 62 to Newland Avenue on 3 October 1937.
Service 63 to Beverley Road/Endike Lane on 4 July 1938.
Service 64 to Holderness Road on 18 February 1940.
Service 69 to Anlaby Road on 6 September 1942.
Service 70 to Hessle Road, on 1 July 1945.

Hull Corporation Transport had the idea of using one-man-operated trolleybuses. The General Manager at the time, Mr George Henry Pulfrey, worked in conjunction with the bodybuilders, Charles H. Roe of Leeds, who designed a new trolleybus with one-man operation in mind. These new vehicles had two sets of doors; one immediately in front of the front wheels (this was the entrance) with a second set of doors just in front of the rear wheels which were to be the exit doors. They also had two staircases and were built on a Sunbeam MF2B chassis. The first such prototype vehicle, No. 101, was officially named the 'Uniflow' trolleybus and was exhibited at the 1952 Earls Court Motor Show.

Vehicle No. 101 entered the Hull fleet in February 1953 and operated on all the trolleybus routes for a six-week period. Further orders were placed for this model and 102-116 (RKH 102-116) entered service in 1954/5. These trolleybuses became known as the 'Coronation' class as Princess Elizabeth had only recently been crowned Queen. As the idea was to operate these vehicles on a 'pay as you enter' basis, a fare box was fitted to No. 116 for trials but was never actually operated in service as such.

In 1959 a decision was made on replacing the trolleybus routes with buses. On 28 February 1961, the first route was converted to bus operation, this being the 70 service, followed by service 69 on 3 February 1962, service 61 on 28 July 1962, route 64 on 21 September 1963, service 62 on 16 November 1963. The final trolleybus service to be converted to bus operation was the 63 to Endike Lane on 31 October 1964.

A double-deck tram belonging to the Hull Street Tramways is photographed on the Corporation Pier to Beverley Road route. It is seen coming out of Whitefriagate *c.* 1876 and is passing what was once Junction Place.

Also seen on the Beverley Road horse tram route is car No. 15, built in 1877. The horses worked long hours and often only changed twice a day between early morning and late at night. In 1887 an epidemic of mange was reported after four horses fell in the streets whilst pulling the trams. One horse broke its neck.

Good-bye, farewell and into the history books. Two horses pull car No. 23, built in 1882, into Temple Street depot for the last time on 30 September 1899, the last day of horse tram operation. Note the black flag which was carried on the upper deck.

Above: A fully enclosed trailer and a steam locomotive on the Great Union Street and Hedon Road to Lee Smith Street service, which commenced on 21 May 1889. Operated by The Drypool & Marfleet Steam Tramway Co., a fare of 1d was charged for any distance with a ½d fare for workmen. The steam trams finished in Hull on 13 January 1901.

Below: A map showing the electric tram routes in Hull.

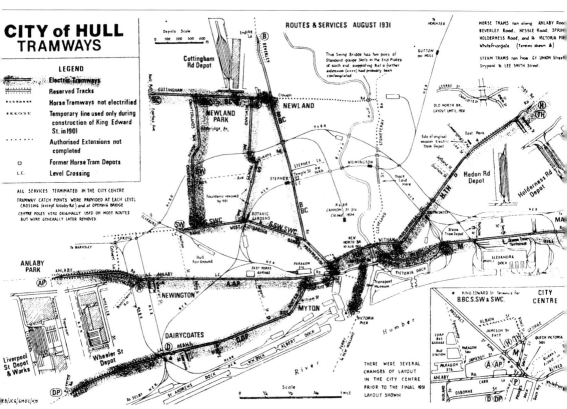

Right: Large crowds gathered in the city centre for the opening of the electric tramway system in Hull on 5 July 1899. Two tram routes operated from St John Street. One to Hessle Road and the other service to Anlaby Road. Tram No. 2 is seen with a full load of passengers. In the background William Wilberforce's Monument is visible.

Below: A policeman looks on as car No. 26 shows itself to the crowds, it was one of fifteen cars built in 1898 by Milnes for the inauguration of the electric tramway system. These cars could carry twenty-eight passengers inside and twenty-two upstairs.

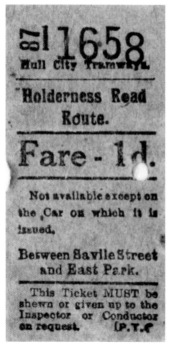

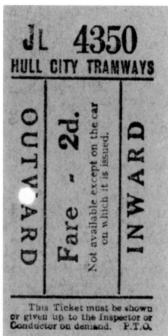

Above: A busy scene in John Street in 1899 looking towards what is now Queen Victoria Square. William Wilberforce's monument can be seen directly in front. Horse-drawn wagons of various sizes, some carrying passengers, are present in great profusion. This was the starting point for the electric trams for Hessle Road and Anlaby Road. The conductor reverses the boom on tram No. 2, built in 1898 for the commencement of tramway operation in Hull the following year.

Left: Two City of Hull Tramways tickets.

THE TRAMS OF HULL

HORSE TRAM ROUTES

Beverley Road	9th January 1875
Spring Bank West	By July 1877
Pier via Whitefriargate	By July 1877
Hessle Road	By July 1877

ELECTRIC TRAM ROUTES

ROUTE	COMMENCED	WITHDRAWN
A Anlaby Road	5th July 1899	5th September 1942
D Hessle Road	5th July 1899	30th June 1945
H Holderness Road	10th April 1900	17th February 1949
S Spring Bank	2nd June 1900	24th July 1937
B Beverley Road	8th December 1900	3rd September 1938
P Pier, Old Town	20th October 1903	5th Sptember 1931
M Hedon Road/Holderness Drain	17th December 1903	1st January 1938
TH Hedon Road via Drypool Bridge	29th July 1907	27th June 1932
SW Spring Bank West	9th October 1913	29th July 1934
DP Dairycoates/Pickering Road	16th February 1914	29th July 1934
BC Beverley Road/Cottingham Road	14th July 1919	29th July 1934
SW Spring Bank/Chanterlands Avenue West (extension)	5th October 1925	29th July 1934
AP Anlaby Road/Pickering Road	5th October 1925	29th July 1934
SWC Spring Bank/Chanterlands Avenue/Cottingham Road	3rd January 1927	29th July 1934

TRAMWAY ROUTE AND EXTENSIONS

Spring Bank Route S	
8th October 1900	Extended to Queens Road
19th January 1903	Extended along Newland Avenue to Cottingham Road
9th October 1913	Branch along Spring Bank West to Walton Street railway level crossing opened as route SW
5th October 1925	Service SW extended along Chanterlands Avenue to Park Avenue
3rd January 1927	Service SW extended along Chanterlands Avenue North to Cottingham Road as route SWC

Holderness Road Route H	
27th March 1903	Extended to Aberdeen Street, in a central reservation.
7th September 1925	Extended to Ings Road
Marfleet Road Route M	
29th April 1912	Extended to Marfleet Avenue
Dairycoates Route D	
16th February 1914	Extended to Pickering Road gates as service DP
5th October 1925	Service DP extended to Pickering Road
Beverley Road Route B	
14th July 1919	Extended to Cottingham Road/Newland Park service BC
5th October 1925	Service BC extended to GoodFellowship Inn
12th July 1926	Service B extended along Beverley Road to Endike Lane, partly on a central reservation
Anlaby Road route A	Extended to Pickering Road in a central reservation as service AP

As can be seen in this photograph, the motorman and the upstairs passengers had no protection against bad weather. The stairs would be very slippery as they were extremely narrow. This photograph was taken at the junction of Cottingham Road and Beverley Road terminus during a cold snap, January 1902.

Passengers for the trams had no worries crossing the roads in those days, as can be seen in this photo of the patrons of tram No. 16 on Anlaby Road. Note the position of the headlight. This photograph was taken on 5 October 1907.

City of Hull Tramways tram No. 31. Built in 1900 by Brush it is seen on the 'A' route to Anlaby Road. The liveries of the trams were maroon and white.

This is Savile Street *c.* 1900 with tram No. 53, built in 1900, travelling along it.

Open top tram No. 16 on the Anlaby Road service in 1899, before the introduction of the large letter boards.

Photographed at Botanic Crossings is tram No. 70 on the 'S' service to Spring Bank. Note how the tram lines had to go into the middle of the road to take the corner. At Botanic crossings you could once catch steam trains to Withernsea and Hornsea.

Photographed in the now-demolished Cottingham Road tram sheds are two semi-enclosed trams. The motorman and the stairs are still open. No. 70 is seen ready to operate the 'B' service to Beverley Road, whilst tram No. 87 will operate the 'S' service to Spring Bank in this 1918 photograph.

The motorman and conductor pose with tram No. 84, ready to operate on the 'MA' service to Marfleet Avenue. This extension of the 'M' route began in April 1912, while the tram itself began life as an open-top vehicle.

In 1903, the first trams arrived with semi-covered roofs. These trams were known as balcony cars. The motorman and conductor pose with tram No. 126 on the 'S' service to Spring Bank.

Four trams can be seen in this photograph taken at the tramway station in Queen Victoria Square. The left tram is on service 'D' to Dairycoates, the middle tram is on route 'A' to Anlaby Road, whilst in the distance a tram is on route 'M' to Marfleet.

Tram No. 65, built in 1900 as an open-top tram, is seen here in its rebuilt form at Queen Victoria tram terminus. The large building facing the camera was the Prudential Tower, which was destroyed during the Second World War. The street on the left is Waterworks Street. Behind the Queen Victoria statue is King Edward Street.

Five trams can be seen in this photograph of King Edward Street on routes 'S' to Spring Bank and on the 'B' route to Beverley Road. Tram No. 79 on the 'S' route shows the moveable top covers fitted between 1903 and 1905, which could be lowered in a form of a roll-top desk, these were the first type of trams to be converted from open-top.

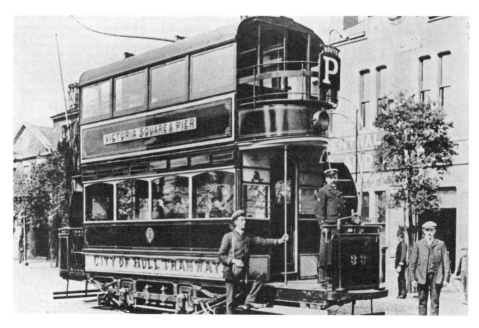

Tram No. 33, built in 1899 as an open-top tram, was later fitted with a top cover as seen in this photograph. It later became a fully-enclosed tram. The conductor and the motorman pose proudly at the Pier terminus.

Besides the cycles and tram No. 106, hardly any other vehicles can be seen on the road. Tram No. 106 is on the 'D' route to Dairycoates, which was the last tram route to be withdrawn. It was withdrawn on 30 June 1945, to be replaced by trolleybus service 70.

Seen on the Beverley Road extension of the route 'B' is tram No. 113 on the 'BC' route to Cottinghan Road. This tram was built by Hull Corporation Transport on Brill 21E trucks. It entered service in 1925.

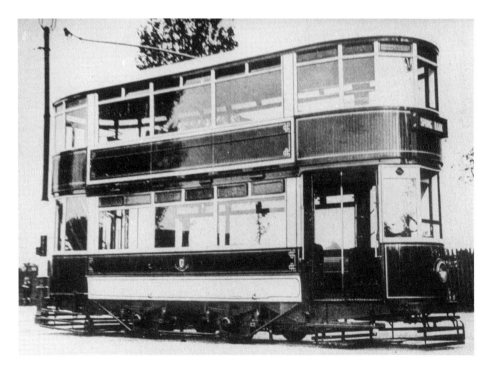

The first tram to be fully enclosed was tram No. 101, built in 1923 by Hull Corporation Transport on EE Rayner trucks. With seating for sixty-six passengers, tram 101 poses for the photographer and is fitted with destination screens.

King Edward Street was the terminus for trams operating on the Beverley Road and Spring Bank routes. In this busy view, tram No. 108 is now fully enclosed on the 'B' route to Beverley Road. Behind is tram No. 5 on the 'S' route to Spring Bank and on the right is tram No. 127.

Two trams, numbers 20 of 1899 and 163 of 1915 (built as a balcony tram), are seen here on the 'D' route to Dairycoates. Note the variation in the livery and also the different position of the headlight.

Horse tram No. 11 is photographed here on the Beverley Road route. It was a large double-deck tram with a seating capacity for forty-four and was built in 1875.

Hull Trams 1875–1945
70 Years of Serving the City

The final tram journey in Hull was on 30 June 1945, when City of Hull Tramways electric tram No. 169, built in 1915, operated the final journey on the 'D' service to Hessle Road. This brought an end to tram services in Hull after seventy years. Tram No. 169 is seen fully illuminated on its last journey.

Trolleybus No. 1 (CRH 925) was the first of twenty-six similar trolleybuses which entered service in 1937 for the 61 route to Chanterlands Avenue north via Spring Bank. The 61 route was opened on 27 July 1937, strangely it replaced a bus service and not a tram route. No. 1 is seen when brand new with the booms on the roof and is photographed before entering service. Note the black on white destination screen and the word 'HULL' proudly displayed on her flank. The destination screen is set for a short working however, and is on service 62A which operated to Newland Avenue.

Photographed on Chanterlands Avenue north is another of the first batch of trolleybuses to enter service in 1937. This is No. 9. Note the slight differences in the livery, gone is the 'HULL' name to be replaced by an advertisement. Also the destination screen is now white on black.

Trolleybus No. 56 (FRH 556), a 1939 utility Leyland TB7 seen on the replacement service 64 to Holderness Road. Trolleybuses replaced trams on this route on 18 February 1940.

Here we see trolleybus No. 80 (GRH 56), a 1945 Sunbeam W with Roe fifty-six-seat bodywork. No. 80 is photographed at the Endike Lane/Beverley Road terminus for service 63. This was the terminus for the old tram route 'B' Note the old telegraph pole and the old-fashioned street lights.

A view inside the now-demolished Cottingham Road depot. The front trolleybus is No. 28 (ERH 28). The advertisements were hand-painted onto the vehicles. No. 28 is a 1938 Crossley TDD4 with Craven fifty-four-seat bodywork. On the right is Coronation class No. 103 (RKH 103), new in 1954. Upon entering the depot, they would first go through the bus wash and then be cleaned inside ready for the next day's service.

Trolleybus No. 47 (FRH 547), a 1939 East Lancs, fifty-four-seat Leyland TB7, is seen on the 64 service to Holderness Road. Trolleybus 47 is photographed on Ferensway outside the railway station. On the left is a once familiar sight, the old Guinness clock. Note how quiet Ferensway is.

The Christmas lights are on in Jameson Street as trolleybus No. 55 (FRH 555), another of the 1939 batch of Leylands, is heading towards Holderness Road on service 64. Behind is East Yorkshire Motor Services No. 496, a 1949 Leyland Titan with Roe Beverley Bar bodywork.

The trolleybuses operated every few minutes and you would often see two or more following each other, as can be seen in this photograph. The leading trolleybus is No. 69 (GRH 289) a utility Brush-bodied Sunbeam W, behind is No. 84, a Roe-bodied Sunbeam W. Visible in the background is an ex-Newcastle Corporation Transport Daimler CVG6

Trolleybus No. 68 (GRH 288) is passing the old P.R. Davis men's outfitters store, which was located under the City Hall. Trolleybus No. 68 is just about to turn right into Carr Lane on the Hessle Road, on the route of service 70.

Travelling up Carr Lane past the old Imperial Hotel is trolleybus No. 96 (HRH 96), one of the last batches to be built to this old style with the entrance at the rear. This trolleybus is a Sunbeam F4 with a Roe body. It is one of the batch of trolleybuses numbers 91–100 to be built to the new width of 8ft. Note the poster on the right from the Trafalgar Street Church.

The 68 service did not in fact go anywhere near Princes Avenue as shown in the destination screen of trolleybus No. 60 (FRH 560). The destination screen is being changed and is being closely watched by the conductor as it gets changed to the correct destination. Another conductor has time for a quick smoke before he takes his next trolleybus out in service.

Photographed on Anlaby Road is trolleybus No. 99 (HRH 99) heading back to the city centre. Service 69 operated between Waterworks Street (renamed Paragon Street), Anlaby Road to Boothferry Road and later extended to Meadowbank Road. Trolleybus No. 99 is an 8ft Sunbeam F4 with Roe sixty-seat bodywork.

Passing down Carr Lane with the old Imperial Hotel on the left, is trolleybus No. 85 (HRH 85), a 1947 Sunbeam W with a Roe rear-entrance bodywork. It is seen on the 69 service to Anlaby Road, this service replacing tram route 'A' on 6 September 1942. The City Hall is seen in the background.

The starting point for the 70 service to Hessle Road was Paragon Street, (it used to be called Waterworks Street). Trolleybus No. 67 (GRH 287), a wartime utility Sunbeam W with a Brush body, is seen here in the city centre. The trolleybuses were built to a very angular outline with no curves and one-piece destination screen. The City Hall can be seen behind No. 67.

During the Second World War Hammonds' store was completely destroyed. Trolleybus No. 54, another of the 1939 Leyland TB7's, is photographed on service 64 during the rebuilding of the store. Note the temporary trolleybus stands.

This 1939 Leyland TB7 with an East Lancs body is photographed passing the Municipal Offices on George Street. No. 66 (FRH 566) is seen heading towards the city centre on the 64 service from Holderness Road. Pedestrians can be seen just behind the trolleybus and are running in front of the oncoming motorbus.

The first 'Coronation' class trolleybus to enter the Hull Corporation fleet was No. 101 (NRH 101). This prototype was built in 1953 and the idea was to operate these vehicles on a one-man basis, using a fare box. Due to Union disapproval it was never used in service as a one-man-operated trolleybus. 101 is seen turning round Queen Victoria Square on the 63 route.

THE CORONATION CLASS
Fleet numbers 101–116
Reg. Numbers NRH 101/
    RKH 102–116
Year built 1952& 1954/5
Year Withdrawn 1964
Chassis: Sunbeam MF2B
Bodywork: Roe 54 seats

Coronation Class No. 104 is seen here outside Cottingham Road depot on the last day of Trolleybus operation. The board in the window reads:

The last day of trolley buses
1937–1964
Oct. 31st

These trolleybuses had only a short working span with Hull Corporation Transport when they were eventually withdrawn and sent for scrap and the whole fleet of buses were between only nine and twelve years old.

four

Hull's Buses 1909-1969: The First Sixty Years

Motorbuses started their operations in Hull on 31 July 1909, operated by the City of Hull Tramways with a service between New Cleveland Street and Stoneferry Green. Six second-hand Saurer, open-top, thirty-four-seat, double-deck buses were acquired from the Mersey Railway Co. This service suffered from unreliable vehicles and high maintenance costs, so it was withdrawn in 1912.

Nine years after the Stoneferry service was withdrawn, a new service from Bond Street to Stoneferry Green began using more reliable AEC K type motorbuses, one was a single-deck, thirty-three-seater (numbered 1), while the two double-deck models with open top and open staircase were numbered 2 and 3 with seating for forty-six passengers. More buses were purchased in 1923 and these included nine Bristol 4-ton motorbuses and one Guy BA bought for new services to Garden Village on 28 March 1923. These buses were earmarked for use on the service to Fish Dock (starting on 15 October 1923) and to New Bridge Road (commencing on 23 October 1923) and were also regularly used on the service along Boothferry Road which began on 31 December 1927.

Bus services supplemented the tram routes and as buses did not need tracks to operate on, they were able to travel beyond the tram terminus. Still, these early buses were, to say the least, very uncomfortable vehicles with solid wheels while double-deck buses had an open-top and open staircase. Although pneumatic tyres were soon fitted and later buses would eventually be fully enclosed, this was not to happen for a number of years.

In the 1920s several other bus operators were running bus services out of Hull city centre. One such service was provided by J.B. McMasters, who operated a Hull to Hessle service which came to be purchased by City of Hull Tramways in January 1923, but, as that company could not operate outside the city boundary, it was then sold to Hull City Motor Works in August 1923.

Two other important bus operators in the Hull area were Lee & Beaulah Ltd which had started running buses in 1921, and Hull & District Motor Services Ltd, which began three years later, both serving the villages surrounding Hull.

On 5 October 1926, East Yorkshire Motor Services was formed as a result of an agreement between Lee & Beaulah Ltd, Hull & District Motor Services Ltd and the British Automobile Traction Co. Ltd. The old East Yorkshire Motor Services livery of royal blue and primrose was also the livery of the old Lee & Beaulah Co., thus East Yorkshire Motor Services retained these colours until it became part of the National Bus Co. and buses were painted poppy red in the 1970s.

East Yorkshire Motor Services purchased other bus operators in 1926 in the area. These included Laidlaw's Motors (which operated between Hull and Hedon), D.W. Burn, (Hull to Withernsea), and N. Thompson (on a Hull to Sutton and Preston service). Although further bus operators were acquired in 1927-1928, these three represented the core of the company's new business.

In 1932, Hull Corporation Transport introduced a service-numbering scheme, previously, coloured lights were used to distinguish between the various bus services while, also in the same year, the livery was changed on motorbuses from crimson lake and white to azure blue and white. This remaining the standard colour scheme for many years. In 1936 the streamlined livery was introduced.

In 1934 the co-ordination agreement between East Yorkshire Motor Services and Hull Corporation Transport came into effect. This allowed for better co-ordination of bus services. Under the agreement two operating areas were introduced: 'A' area (inner) and the 'B' area (suburban). In the 'A' area all the revenue collected went to the Corporation, whilst in the 'B' area the revenue was shared between the two operators. Both Hull Corporation Transport and

East Yorkshire Motor Services used different tickets for each area, with tickets marked with either an 'A' or 'B'.

However, the introduction of the co-ordination agreement did lead directly to the early demise of trams in Hull. East Yorkshire Motor Services had a big problem with double-deck buses on its services beyond Beverley towards Driffield and York. All buses going past Beverley had to pass under a pointed Gothic arch known as the Beverley Bar. Normal height double-deck buses could not pass under this arch because the arch was rounded at the top and the sides sloped inwards. Most of the double-deck fleet had specially tapered roofs to cope with this problem and these buses were known as 'Beverley Bar buses'. The first such vehicles to join the East Yorkshire Motor Services fleet entered service in 1934.

As new housing estates were built on the outskirts of the city, the fleet of the Hull Corporation Transport grew. At the end of 1935 the fleet totalled 110 vehicles, but, by the end of 1940, this had increased to 139. Hull's status as a centre of industry meant that the city would be targeted in wartime and thus all vehicles were under great risk of attack. Indeed, during the Second World War, the blitz on Hull led to a number of the Corporation's buses being destroyed. In one night, 7 May 1941, the central bus garage and head office were completely destroyed along with forty-four motorbuses. The overhead wires of the trolleybuses and trams were also brought down by enemy bombs. Both East Yorkshire Motor Services and Hull Corporation Transport took delivery of very basic 'utility' buses during the war, they were on Guy Arab chassis and had an angular profile body that saved many hours of panel-beating.

After the war, expansion of both fleets continued, and new, more modern buses were purchased. East Yorkshire Motor Services bought a number of low-height buses over the years. The need for buses to be built to low height was necessary in order for double-deck buses to be able to get underneath several of the railway bridges in the East Riding. These were strange vehicles, especially upstairs, as seats were in a single row of four, whilst the gangway, which had to be full-height for the passengers to walk down, was sunken to the rest of the upper deck. Passengers had to step up from the sunken gangway and slide along four seats to the window. Downstairs, with the gangway-sunken, passengers on the right-hand side of the bus had reduced headroom. It was not uncommon for passengers leaving their seats to forget to lower their heads first.

On 18 January 1954, Hull Corporation Transport introduced one-man-operation buses using two converted AEC Regal single-deck buses. Further to this, one-man-operated, single-deck buses were purchased in 1957 while East Yorkshire Motor Services continued to purchase rear entrance, single-deck buses in the 1950s. The job of converting sixteen of the 1952 batch of rear entrance, single-deck buses to front entrance was carried out between 1959 and 1962 by Charles H. Roe of Leeds. In their new disguise they were suitable for one-man-operation.

Hull Corporation Transport was an early user of the then modern rear-engined bus, the Leyland Atlantean. The company purchased its first such buses in 1960 while East Yorkshire Motor Services stayed faithful to the front-engined, double-deck buses, taking their last batch as late as 1966, most of these buses were fitted with the Beverley Bar Roofline. Its first rear-engined double-deck entered service in 1967. On 29 January 1961 trolleybus route 70 to Hessle Road was the first trolleybus route to be converted to bus operation, and gradually all trolleybus routes were converted to motorbus operation, this process eventually being completed in 1964.

One-man operation was extended to the use of double-deck buses by Hull Corporation Transport on 14 September 1969, while it was also in 1969 that East Yorkshire Motor Services became a member of the National Bus Co.

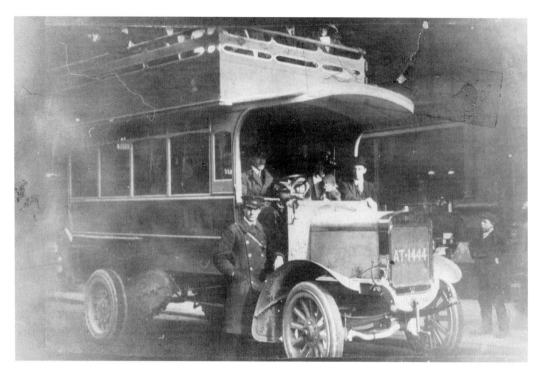

Comfort on the very early motorbuses was an alien concept, as can be seen by this early open-top double-deck bus with solid wheels. It was working on a service from Hull in the early 1900s.

Opposite above: The Red Chara operated these two early char-a-bancs on services from Hull, including the Hull to Beverley service. The drivers pose proudly with AT 7873 and AT 7832.

Opposite below: City of Hull Tramways began its first bus service in 1909, using six Saurer buses with Brown & Hughes thirty-four-seat open top/open staircase. One of the six is seen here. The service proved to be short-lived and was eventually withdrawn in 1912.

A 1921 AEC 'K' (AT 2934), part of the fleet of Hull City Tramways. Here we see one of the three AEC 'K's purchased for the service between Bond Street and Stoneferry Green.

In 1923 City of Hull Tramways purchased this Bristol 4 ton with English Electric fifty-three-seat body, also equipped with an open-top and outside staircase. No. 4 (AT 7353) is on the Stoneferry service, whilst a tram is seen on the Spring Bank service.

Another Bristol 4-ton motorbus, this model was part of the fleet of City of Hull Tramways. This is No. 8 (AT 8381) new in 1923, and is a fifty-four-seat bus with an English Electric body. Despite recent technological developments this model still had solid wheels, a staircase in the open and an open-top roof.

Lee & Beulah Ltd was running this Leyland char-a-banc on an excursion to Bridlington. This company began running buses in 1921.

Here we see another vehicle in the Lee & Beulah Ltd fleet, a Leyland with a Leyland twenty-six-seat body (BT 5599). This bus formed part of the East Yorkshire Motor Services fleet in 1926.

This twenty-nine-seat Dennis was one of the many buses taken over by East Yorkshire Motor Services. Details about EYMS No. 53 (BT 9889) are not known. However, it is known that it was acquired in 1926.

Enterprise operated this open-top, double-deck bus on a service between Hull and Cottingham. Enterprise was taken over by East Yorkshire Motor Services. WF 88 model is seen here with the conductor and driver.

Returning to the city centre is an East Yorkshire Motor Services Leyland Lion PLSC3 with thirty-two-seat bodywork. Delivered to EYMS in 1928, No. 79 (WF 1152) was the first new bus to be purchased by the new company.

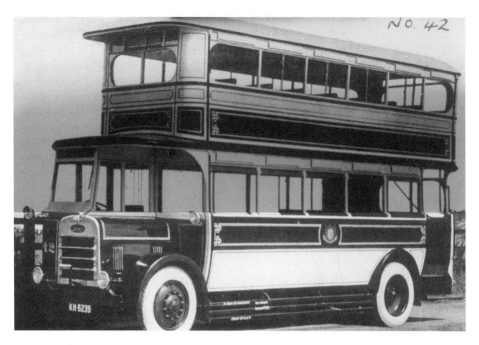

The City of Hull Tramways purchased six Bristol A's in 1928 with covered top built by Roe. One of the six is No. 42 (KH 6239) with the unusual top clearly visible. The top did not extend over the drivers cab. It is also fitted with pneumatic tyres and an enclosed staircase.

East Yorkshire Motor Services purchased large numbers of Leylands. On the right is No. 135 (KH 7949), a 1929 Leyland Titan TD1 with a Leyland forty-eight-seat body. On the left is No. 119, (KH 6986) a 1929 Tilling Stevens B10A.

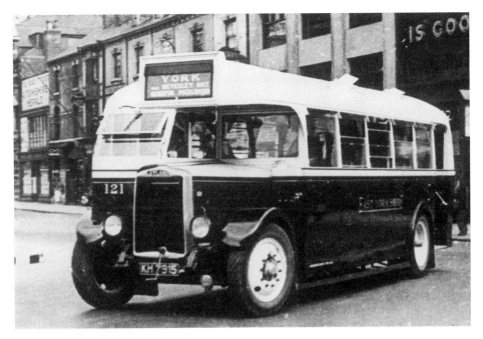

Another Leyland bus: No. 121 (KH 7915) a Leyland Tiger TS2 with a smart Hall & Lewis twenty-five-seat, rear entrance saloon. It is photographed leaving Paragon Square on the service to York.

Parked in Paragon Square is East Yorkshire Motor Services No. 139 (KH 7953) a 1929 Leyland Titan TD1 with Leyland open staircase and fifty-one-seat bodywork. This bus is seen on the Hessle service while behind the Paragon Music Store is clearly visible; Note the poster on the side of the bus, HULL TO WITHERNSEA DAY RETURN 1s 9d.

Left: Kingston upon Hull Corporation Transport purchased ten AEC Regals in 1932 with Brush and English Electric bodies which they then numbered 1-10. No. 8 (RH 4757) is an English-Electric-bodied vehicle. It is seen here in St John Street, now known as Carr Lane. In the background is William Wilberforce's Monument. While on the right is the once well-known Hull store of Willis's. The AEC Regal is on a service to the Fish Dock on service 1.

Below: East Yorkshire Motor Services No. 208 (BT 9980) was one of the vehicles acquired with the Binnington Motors Ltd fleet in 1932. It is a 1926 Leyland Lion PLSC1 with a Leyland thirty-one-seat front entrance.

Above: Another ex-Binnington Leyland Titan TD2 is No. 229 (WF 4735) with its new Brush Beverley Bar body replacing the original Strachan & Brown body. No. 229 is photographed at Hessle Square with the Granby pub in the background.

Right: The driver poses in front of Binnington Motors Ltd No. 44 (WF 3828), a forty-eight-seat all-Leyland Titan TD1 which was new in 1932.

East Yorkshire Motor Services No. 245 ((RH 8914), a 1934 Leyland Titan TD3 with a Brush fifty-two-seat body, is photographed in Paragon Square on a service to Withernsea via the Aerodrome, Hedon and Patrington. East Yorkshire Motor Services operated from the city streets and did not transfer their services to the new bus station until 1937.

Hull Corporation Transport bus No. 2, a 1932 AEC Regal with Brush thirty-one-seat body is seen here on 8 May 1941, the day after Hull took a severe bombing from the German bombers. The ruins of the bus garage can be seen behind the bus. Forty-three motorbuses were destroyed in the raid. Note the sign on the lamp post, the S and arrow is indicating the way to an air raid shelter.

East Yorkshire Motor Services No. 275 (AKH 763). The first buses fitted with the Beverley Bar roofs entered the fleet in 1934. 275 is a Leyland Titan TD4 with Brush bodywork. It shows the strange shape of the roofs on these buses which were needed to pass underneath the Bar at Beverley.

East Yorkshire Motor Services No. 280 (AKH 768), a 1935 English Electric thirty-seat-bodied Leyland Tiger TS7, is seen here on a service to Cottingham. A bemused gentleman sits in the vehicle as he glares at the photographer.

Hull Corporation Transport 156 (CAT 157), a 1936 Daimler COG5 with a Weymann body, is photographed at the busy junction of Jameson and Prospect Streets. In the background are two trams on the 'B' and 'S' services. This streamlined livery was introduced in 1936.

The coach station (demolished in 2005) was opened on 22 October 1935. However, East Yorkshire Motor Services did not actually transfer their buses to the new coach station until 1937. Four double-deck buses, three of them with the Beverley Bar roof, can be seen in this photograph; No. 401 (GKH 697) a 1943 Guy Arab II with its new Roe body; behind is No. 422 (HAT 638) a 1947 Leyland Titan PD1, also with a Roe body. The 422 is on the service to Hornsea. Neither of these two services passed under Beverley Bar.

Three Hull Corporation Transport double-deck buses can be seen here lined up at the back of the bus station. On the left are numbers 191 (GKH 372) and 193. Both are 1942 AEC Regents, originally they were equipped with the Brush utility body they received at manufacture. They received these 1939 Massey body's in 1950. On the right is No. 209 (GKH 932), a 1943 Guy Arab 1. Originally equipped with a Massey fifty-seat utility body, it received this 1937 Weymann body in 1949.

During the Second World War Hull Corporation Transport were allocated a number of buses, which had mainly been intended for other fleets. Four vehicles were diverted from Western S.M.T., Kilmarnock, in 1942 (numbers 200-203). They were Leyland Titan TD7's with Leyland's own bodywork. One of the batch is No. 203 (GKH 384). These vehicles retained the Scottish destination screen. Note the position of the service number.

The utility buses were very basic. They had very square bodywork, saving hours of panel-beating, and had wooden slatted seats fitted. No. 236 (GRH 381) is seen with the conductor changing the destination screen. No. 236 is a 1945 Guy Arab II with a Massey body.

East Yorkshire Motor Services standard double-deck buses had Beverley Bar bodies, No. 498 (JAT 466) being no exception. It is a 1949 Leyland Titan PD1 with a Roe body. On the right is No. 555 (LRH 697), a 1951 Brush-bodied Leyland Royal Tiger No. 498 with destination screen indicating a service to Cottingham Green via Derringham Bank and Willerby Inst.

Returning to the city centre from Ellerburn Avenue on the 22 service we can see Hull Corporation Transport bus No. 242 (HAT 242). Among the first of the post-war buses to be purchased by the Corporation, it is a Weymann sixty-seat-bodied AEC Regent II. Behind it is No. 336 (OKH 336), a 1953 AEC Regent III with Weymann fifty-eight-seat bodywork, seen passing the old Mayfair Cinema on the right whilst on the left is Coronation class trolleybus No. 106.

For use on tours, express work and normal services is East Yorkshire No. 499 seen here at the rear of the bus station. It was among a number of Leyland Tiger PS1s with thirty-one-seat Eastern Coachworks bodywork that were purchased in 1948.

East Yorkshire Motor services No. 522 (KKH 875) was a touring service, a function which came to be performed by the Leyland Tiger PS2/3, a vehicle with a front sliding door which was delivered to the company in 1950. They were used on tours and express work, with the coachwork having been provided by Burlingham.

Two of East Yorkshire's Leyland Titan's with Beverley Bar roofs. No. 484 (JAT 452) was new in 1949, behind it is 547 (LAT 75) of 1950, both buses have bodywork by Roe. No. 484 has its destination screen already changed for its next run to Withernsea, whilst 547 has just returned from Hornsea.

The first single-deck buses delivered to Hull Corporation Transport for many years were six AEC Regal III''s, with Weymann thirty-five-seat front entrance bodies delivered in 1949. One of the six is No. 2 (KKH 647), seen here in the bus station before embarking on service 19 to Sutton Road. They were converted to one-man operation in 1954 and fitted with power-operated doors.

The first 8ft-wide buses for the Corporation also arrived in 1949, they were AEC Regent III's with Weymann fifty-eight-seat bodies numbered 280-315 (KAT 290-315). One of the batch, No. 296, is seen here heading back to the city centre.

A busy scene in the Coach Station. The front bus is Hull Corporation Transport No. 341 (OKH 341), a 1953 AEC Regent III with Weymann concealed radiator fifty-eight-seat body. Behind is AEC Regal No. 6, at the rear of No. 6 is No. 533, a 1950 Roe-bodied Leyland Titan in the East Yorkshire fleet. There is an interesting contrast between the side advertisements on the front buses, one advertises milk whilst the other advertises Cream Label Stout!

In 1952 East Yorkshire Motor Services purchased a batch of sixteen Leyland Royal Tigers with Roe forty-two-seat rear entrance bodies. One of the batch, No. 593 (MKH 411) is seen here. This batch were converted to front entrance between 1959 and 1962 and used as one-man-operated buses.

East Yorkshire Motor Services took a batch of Leyland Titan PD2/12's with standard EYMS Roe fifty-six-seat Beverley Bar buses in 1953. No. 611 (NRH 222) is on a service to Hessle Square via Hessle Road. The old ABC cinema (now demolished) is in the background.

Also delivered to East Yorkshire Motor Services in 1953 were three Leyland Royal Tigers with distinctive Windover coach bodies, still with rear entrance bodies. No. 613 (NRH 654), the first of the batch, is seen here in later years operating on normal bus services. Behind is a 'Bluebottle' Leyland Titan, and just visible behind the coach is an early AEC Bridgemaster.

East Yorkshire Motor Services changed to AEC's in 1956 for its double-deck buses. This Willowbrook fifty-six-seat Regent V with the Beverley Bar roof is seen here in Hull Coach Station. No. 644 (VKH 44) is now preserved by the company and is available for private hire.

Hull Corporation Transport's first real one-man-operated, single-deck buses were delivered in 1957. No. 66, an AEC Reliance with Weymann thirty-nine-seat body, dual doorway, is seen on service 19 to Sutton Road. No. 66 is photographed after passing underneath the railway bridge on Beverley Road. A 'Coronation' trolleybus is seen behind on the 63 service to Endike Lane.

It was once common for East Yorkshire coaches to be named, this is No. 678 (WAT 678), which was named *Buckrose Star*. Delivered to the company in 1957, it is a thirty-five-seat Harrington-bodied Leyland Tiger Cub. These coaches were used on extended coach tours. The board on the right displays the following notice; '1965 Round Britain in comfort with East Yorkshire'.

One of the Author's favourite East Yorkshire Motor Services buses is seen here at speed on a Leeds express service. This is No. 681 (6681 KH), a 1960 M.C.W forty-one-seat Leyland Tiger Cub. These buses looked very smart in this livery.

East Yorkshire Motor Services purchased the new AEC Bridgemaster with Park Royal seventy-six-seat bodies in 1960. The first Bridgemasters did not have the Beverley Bar roof or sloping upper-deck windows. Here we see No. 696 (6696 KH) leaving the coach station on a service to South Cave.

This is an example of a later AEC Bridgemaster with the sloping inward upper deck windows. No. 708 (4708 AT) was new in 1961 and carries a Park Royal seventy-three-seat rear entrance body. Behind is No. 855, a 1968 Daimler Fleetline also with sloping upper deck windows. They are both passing the railway station and are about to turn into the bus station.

Hull Corporation Transport was an early user of the new, modern Leyland Atlantean and purchased its first batch in 1960. These PDR1/1's had seventy-five-seat bodies by MCCW. No. 342 (6342 KH) is photographed here when still new. Note the entrance sign on the first lower deck window, whilst the notice in the windscreen reads 'FRONT ENTRANCE ONLY'.

Hull Corporation Transport bought a number of Leyland Panthers with attractive Roe forty-four or forty-five-seat dual doorway bodies between 1964 and 1966. No. 172 (GAT 172D) was the first of the batch. It is seen here alongside the preserved No. 64 (WAT 164), a 1957 Weymann-bodied AEC Reliance. Both are seen at Stagecoach's 1999 open day to mark the one-hundredth anniversary of City of Hull Tramways' establishment in 1899.

The East Yorkshire Co. bought this Leyland Panther with Marshall forty-nine-seat body in 1966. No. 803 (GAT 803D) is seen here on the mud at the rear of the bus station with the destination screen set for an express service to Hornsea.

East Yorkshire Motor Services remained faithful to the front-engined bus, taking its last batch of such vehicles as late as 1966. No. 815 (GAT 815D), a 1966 AEC Renown with a Park Royal sixty-eight-seat body, is seen here on a service from York to Bridlington.

Hull Corporation Transport took delivery of twenty Leyland Atlanteans with Roe seventy-one-seat dual doorway in 1969. One of the batch is No. 276 (TKH 276H), seen here turning into Ferensway from Carr Lane. East Yorkshire No. 756 (3756 RH), a 1963 AEC Bridgemaster, is behind.

The first rear-engined, double-deck buses for East Yorkshire Motor Services did not enter service until 1967. These were Daimler Fleetlines with Park Royal sixty-eight-seat bodywork. No. 871 (RAT 871G) is a 1969 vehicle. No. 871 is seen sandwiched between two AEC Regents, No. 644 is seen on the right.

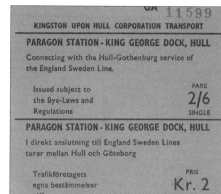

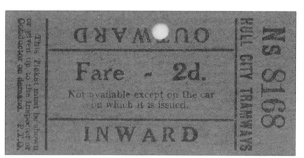

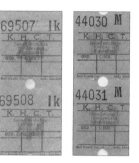

Above: The first bus to have the Beverley Bar roof was No. 270 (RH 9698), a 1934 Leyland Titan TD3 with Brush fifty-one-seat bodywork. Note the unusual three-window design. No. 270 is photographed on the return journey from Scarborough to Bridlington and would have to go under the Bar at Beverley before coming back to Hull.

Below: This is Beverley Bar bus No. 367 (ERH 361), a 1938 Leyland Titan again with Brush bodywork. It is seen here heading towards Hull, again proudly exhibiting the unusual windows on its upper deck.

Photographed on Beverley Road at the junction of Endike Lane, Beverley Bar bus No. 472 (JAT 440), a 1949 Leyland Titan with a Roe fifty-four-seat body, is heading towards Beverley. Two Hull Corporation Transport 'Coronation' class trolleybuses are seen on the 63 service. On the right is No. 103. This is the turning point for trolleybuses on this route.

A cyclist prepares to overtake Beverley Bar bus No. 511 (JRH 984), a 1949 Leyland Titan with Roe bodywork. Behind is either No. 651 or 652, both EYMS Beverley Bar buses, but this one is a 1957 AEC Regent V with a Roe body.

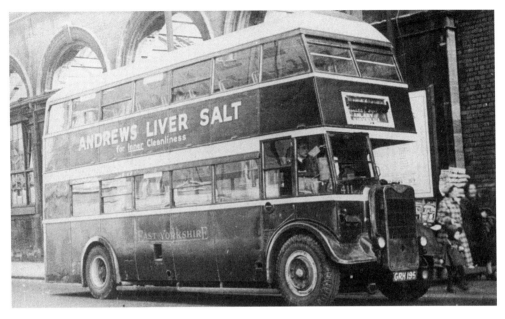

The utility buses were very square-looking, but this design saved many hours of panel-beating. Seen here at Hull Coach Station is No. 411 (GRH195) built in 1944. It is a Guy Arab II and is seen with its original Brush body. It was later re-bodied by Roe.

This is No. 573, a 'Yellow Peril' squeezing underneath the Beverley Bar with only inches to spare. No. 573 was one of a number of Leyland Titans with Roe dual-purpose seating to be purchased in 1952, the majority of which were painted in dual-purpose livery. Note the 10ft 9in headroom notice.

In 1956 a batch of AEC Regent V's with Willowbrook fifty-six-seat bodywork entered the fleet, again fitted with the traditional Beverley roof and sloping upper-deck windows. One of the batch, No. 645 (VKH 45), is leaving the now-demolished bus station in Hull on a service to Bridlington via Beverley and the Beverley Bar.

The later buses built for use to go under the Beverley Bar did not have 'pointed' roofs, as these newer vehicles were chassis-less with sub-frames at the front and rear. These new buses were known as the Bridgemasters. Those destined for East Yorkshire had standard bodies except that the upper deck windows sloped inwards, as seen here with No. 718 (9718 AT), shown with an AEC front entrance body, which was new in 1962 and is seen with the 'clippie' on the No. 2 service.

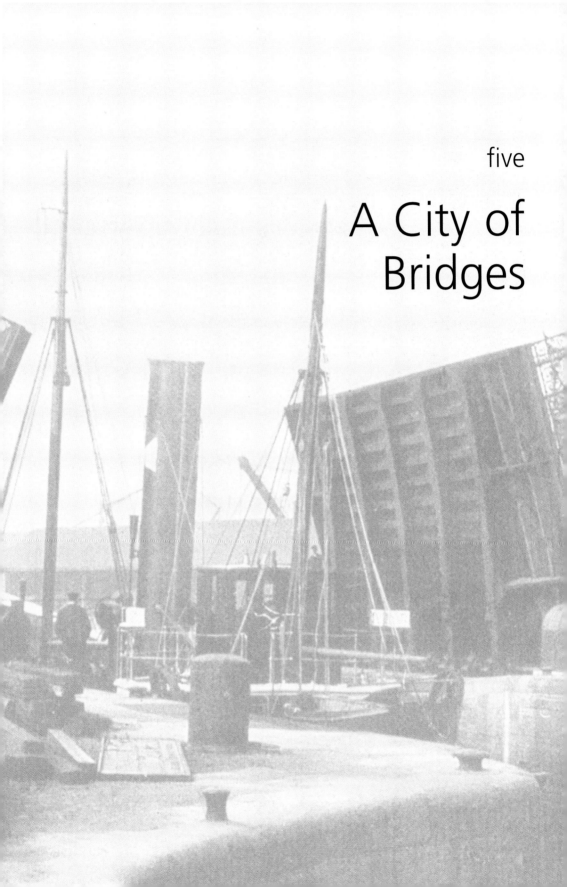

five

A City of
Bridges

The bridges over the River Hull are a dominant feature of Hull's landscape. From the early days it was necessary to cross the River Hull from the east side to the west side of the river. As early as 1541 a bridge was built just to the south of the present North bridge, this bridge remained in use until 1870, although it was modified and rebuilt at one time or another. It was approached via Charlotte Street and was finally replaced by a new bridge in 1870, this itself was replaced by the present North bridge in 1931. This bridge, officially opened on 10 August 1893, was much wider than the old bridge and joined Holderness Road, Witham, with George Street and the city centre.

The South bridge joined the old town to the many timber yards of Hull as well as the Victoria Dock. Indeed, the volume was such that at one time a toll was charged to cross it and so it came to be known as 'Ha'Penny bridge', South bridge was built in 1865 and demolished in 1944.

Further up the River Hull, with the city expanding outside the old town walls, a further bridge was added in 1874. This was Sculcoates bridge, (known to many as Chapman Street bridge) built by Darlaston contractors and the Bridge & Roofing Co. Ltd. J. Fox. Sharp was the engineer. This is the oldest bridge still in use over the River Hull.

In 1888 a new bridge was built, this was Drypool bridge, a narrow bridge which joined Alfred Gelder Street with Clarence Street and Holderness Road. This bridge remained in use until the new Drypool bridge was built in 1961. The much-needed railway bridge finally became a reality when a single track bridge was built in 1853 for the York & North Midland Railway, this was the Wilmington railway bridge and it remained in use until it was replaced by a new bridge built for the North Eastern Railway. This bridge was opened on 10 May 1907, and although no longer used by the railways it remains in use as a footpath across the river. In 1885 a large girder railway bridge was built which connected many of the freight tracks to and from the docks, and no doubt its builders would be pleased to learn that it is still in use today.

In 1901 a small bridge joining Scott Street, Wincolmlee with Jenning Street was built. The approach to the bridge from Scott Street and Wincolmlee and was very tight for vehicles intending to cross, especially in later years as horse-drawn carts gave way to motorised vehicles. Scott Street bridge opened for traffic in 1902. This bridge is no longer in use and is now permanently in the 'up' position,

In 1905 a new bridge was built, this was Stoneferry bridge which linked Clough road with Stoneferry, and the growing industrial area which became known as the Stoneferry Industrial Estate. A new, ultra-modern, two-lane bridge replaced the old bridge in 1991 while, as Hull continued to grow to the north of the town centre and new houses were built, a new road-bridge was built on Sutton Road in 1937 linking Beverley Road with East Hull, Holderness Road, and Hedon Road.

Sutton Road bridge was the last bridge to be built over the River Hull for many years and, until a new road, the Clive Sullivan Way was built, this new road took traffic from the A63 and by-passed the city centre. The Myton bridge was built in 1979 to cross over the River Hull. Incidentally this bridge was built very close to where the South bridge once stood over sixty years ago. Further development north of the city centre saw new housing estates develop in the 1990s, and although it was originally hoped to serve these areas by way of a tunnel under the River Hull, and work actually began on the construction, the tunnel flooded on a number of occasions, and so it was decided to build another bridge instead.

This bridge, the Ennerdale link road bridge, linked traffic from the A1079, Beverley by-pass and traffic from Beverley to the new Kingswood Park development and Bransholme. This bridge opened in 1997 and is a dual-carriageway road bridge. The final bridge to be built was the Millennium footbridge, completed in 2001 which links the old town to the very impressive Hull attraction that is the world's only submarium, 'The Deep'.

The many ships which once sailed from all over the world to Hull would sail the last twenty-five miles down the River Humber from the North Sea and, wanting to dock in one of the towns docks, would firstly enter the Humber Dock basin before entering Humber Dock (built in 1809). Vessels which wished to dock in Queens's Dock, which was completed in 1778, would first have to pass underneath Mytongate bridge and into Junction Dock, (built in 1829 and later named Princes Dock in 1854) and then underneath Monument bridge which was built in 1906 and past the monument of William Wilberforce and the Dock offices on the left before sailing into Queens Dock.

Ships wishing to berth in Railway Dock (built in 1846) would enter the Humber Dock and turn to port underneath the Railway Dock bridge into Railway Dock to moor-up and discharge their cargo. With the arrival of the railways into the city in the mid-1800s the amount of freight being transported to and from the new docks on the eastern side of the city grew. In consequence the Hull & Barnsley Railway built railway lines on embankments high above ground level. These crossed over many of Hull's main roads, including Boothferry Road, Anlaby Road, Chanterlands Avenue, Beverley Road, Newland Avenue and Holderness Road.

As more branch lines opened up within the city more overhead bridges were built. The use of overhead railway bridges did away with the need for level crossings. Indeed, many of the overhead bridges are still in use today, but with the decline in rail freight and the removal of many railway tracks many more of the overhead bridges were demolished or simply fell into disuse and ruin.

At one time the outskirts of the city had many drains from the fields to take excess water to the River Hull. Many of these have been lost, one drain however remains, this is the Barmston drain, which runs from Beverley, Dunswell and into the outskirts of Hull. The first bridge on which you pass over the drain is on Hall Road, Orchard Park Estate. Like many estates this was farmland until it was built on in the early 1970s. The drain then passes under Greenwood Avenue, Endike Lane, Beverley Road (alongside Inglemire Lane), Clough Road, Sculcoates Lane, Stepney Lane, Fountain Road, Lockwood Street and Wincolmlee before finally running into the River Hull. Some of the bridges over the drain date from the 1880s, whilst other bridges were built at the same time as the building of the North Hull Estate in the 1930s/1940s. Many of the old drains were filled-in over the years whilst the remains of some of the bridges can still be seen to this day.

Boats of various sizes are seen moored-up in this undated photograph of the old Drypool bridge. This
bridge was a wrought iron swing bridge and opened in 1888. This originally joined Salthouse Lane to
Clarence Street. On the right is the old Rank's mill. This was destroyed during the blitz on Hull during
the Second World War. Joseph Rank began milling in this area in 1875.

THE RIVER HULL
AND THE BRIDGES

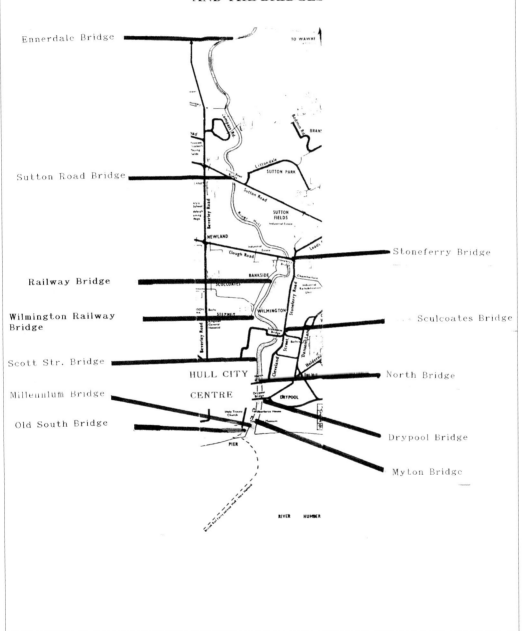

The old Drypool bridge was very narrow as can be seen here with a Hull Corporation Transport double-deck AEC Regent crossing the bridge. With increasing problems caused by the lack of space, this bridge was replaced in 1961 by the present-day bridge.

Looking towards the River Humber and Drypool bridge from the Garrison side of the River Hull, Myton bridge is just visible in the background.

Right: Drypool bridge is lifted to let the pleasure boat *Artic Fern* pass underneath. In the background is Clarence Mill which opened in 1952 replacing the earlier mill.

Below: Don't step back! Bridge operator Bryan Fish greases the mechanism on Drypool bridge. The coaster *Annette J* passes close by.

A Hull Corporation fully enclosed tram is seen crossing North bridge on the 'H' service to Holderness Road. North bridge opened on 10 August 1931.

North bridge is an important bridge as it links the city centre with Holderness Road and then onto east Hull and the suburbs. It carries a vast amount of traffic each day, trams, trolleybuses and buses have crossed this bridge. A Hull Corporation trolleybus crosses the bridge on its return to the city centre.

Two trolleybuses are seen under the girders of North bridge on the 64 service to Holderness Road, returning back to the city centre. The trolleybus wires were carried in trunking in the centre of the bridge as can be seen in this photograph.

North bridge is seen here in the open position undergoing repairs during 2005, repairs which cost at least £1,500,000. This photograph was taken from the Garrison side of the River Hull.

25 OCT 190

The old bridge is in the centre of the photograph whilst work starts on the new Wilmington bridge in the background. Note the vast open areas in the background.

Opposite above: The oldest bridge still to cross the River Hull is Sculcoates bridge (known to many Hull people as Chapman Street bridge). It was built in 1874 and opened in 1875. Built by the Bridge & Roofing Co. Ltd and Darlaston Contractors, Sculcoates bridge links Chapman Street with Swann Street.

Opposite below: Crossing the old Wilmington railway bridge here is steam engine No. 370. This bridge is a single-track bridge and was built for the York & North Midland Railway in 1853.

The erection of the new Wilmington railway bridge was nearly complete at the time of this photograph in April 1907. The new railway bridge was built for the North Eastern Railway and was opened on 10 May 1907, a month after this photograph was taken.

Built in 1905, the elegant Wilmington railway bridge still survives a hundred years later. Although it is no longer used as a railway bridge, it still serves the community as a pedestrian and cycle track.

The old Bridge Master's House at Scott Street bridge.

Looking up-river with the old Scott Street bridge seen in the open position, Scott Street bridge opened on 3 October 1902. This bascule bridge is worked by hydraulic power and was at one time used to connect Scott Street with Jennings Street.

The railway bridge is still in use for freight traffic. Built for the Hull & Barnsley Railway in 1885, it is worked by hydraulic power while a tunnel under the riverbed is used for services.

Opposite below: A view of the River Hull at Stoneferry taken *c.* 1899. A sloop can be seen discharging its cargo for the seed crushers Barton & Warehouse. A small ferry operated between the two sides of the River Hull until the first Stoneferry bridge was opened in 1905.

Right: The old Stoneferry bridge replaced a small ferry service in 1905. This bridge itself was replaced by an ultra-modern bridge in 1991.

Below: The old Stoneferry bridge on Clough Road was a very narrow bridge as can be seen in this undated photograph, but in fact it was wide enough for horse-drawn wagons. A horse-drawn wagon, No. 4, belonging to Robson's Cement of Hull, can be seen in the background.

The old Stoneferry bridge of 1905 was replaced in 1991 with this new, ultra-modern, impressive lift bridge. The bridge is in two separate halves carrying much traffic. The impressive round control tower can also be seen.

Looking east from the river bank the eye falls on the Sutton Road bridge built in 1937. The bridge is an important link as it forms part of the outer ring road for traffic heading towards the docks, P&O Ferries and the east of the city.

The last new road bridge to be built to date is the ultra-modern Ennerdale bridge which opened in 1997. The road is called Raich Carter Way and joins the A1079 Beverley by-pass. It also joins the A1174 road to Beverley and the north, this particular view is taken from the river bank.

An interesting photograph of the mouth of the River Hull. In the foreground the remains of the old Hull Central dry dock are clearly visible while the new Millennium footbridge which opened in 2001 can also be seen, although it is dwarfed by the impressive tidal barrier. The tidal barrier is lowered when there is a risk of flooding to the old town. Just within sight is the Myton bridge.

Myton bridge was built between 1977 and 1979. It was to be known as South bridge until the plans changed. Myton bridge carries the A63 (also called Garrison Road) across the River Hull, near to where the South bridge once stood.

A single motor vehicle can be seen in this undated photograph of Spring Bank West. The overhead railway bridge is advertising Thelson Motor Oils.

The first railway bridge that the train traveller will notice after leaving Hull Paragon Railway Station is Park Street bridge. This photograph looks west towards the bridge, the waste ground in front of it was once occupied by old terraced houses, but they were destroyed during the Second World War.

Hull Corporation trolleybus No. 73, built in 1945, is photographed on the 65 service to Chanterlands Avenue. It is approaching the trolleybus terminus after emerging from the overhead railway bridge. The road under this bridge dips and is often flooded after a downpour.

Boothferry Road railway bridge is in fact two separate girder bridges alongside each other. The impressive girder work is in need of a lick of paint.

The last bridge that the Barmston drain passes underneath before going into the River Hull is Lockwood Street. This bridge is now used purely as a cycle track and footpath.

Built in 1889 this is Fountain Road bridge, which crosses the Barmston drain.

The old swing railway bridge is no longer in use. It used to bridge the railway line of the old lock between the Humber Dock basin and the Humber Dock. The old railway bridge can be clearly seen, Humber Dock was completed in 1809. It is now used as a marina for small luxury boats.

A number of bridges were erected for Hull Corporation over dykes on what is now Bransholme Estate. This is one of them, built by Officers and Men of (East Riding) Field Squadron R.E. (Volunteers of Sutton). This bridge now forms part of the Holwell Road and was erected between 6–14 July 1968.

Victoria Dock was once an important dock on the western side of the River Hull for the landing of wood and other trade. Now most of the dock is filled-in and houses now stand were ships once moored up and the timber yards once stood. This old railway bridge used to swing open. Still visible is the old half-tide basin, while just visible is the outer basin.

Monument bridge seen during its construction in 1906. This linked King Edward Street, St John Street (now called Carr Lane) with Whitefriagate and Alfred Gelder Street. On the right is William Wilberforce's pillar and St John's Church. Other Hull landmarks crossed by Monument bridge were the Junction Dock (later to become Princes Dock after 1854) and Queens Dock.

BRIDGE AND WILBERFORCE MONUMENT, HULL.

Looking across Monument bridge towards St John Street and the City Hall. On the left is William Wilberforce's Monument which was erected in 1834. On the right can be seen the entrance to the old Queens Dock and also the Dock offices which were opened in 1871.

Other local titles published by Tempus

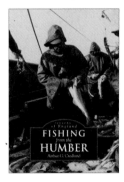

Humber Shipping

ARTHUR G. CREDLAND

Kingston upon Hull has been a major port since medieval times, and over a long period the city grew to be one of Britain's major ports and shipbuilding centres. Today the Humber looks much different than it did even ten years ago. Many docks and warehouses have gone and the fishing fleet is greatly reduced. Illustrated with over 200 images *Humber Shipping* reveals the changing face of the Humber's maritime history.

0-7524-2358-4

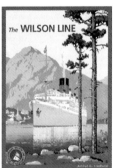

Fishing from the Humber

ARTHUR G. CREDLAND

Illustrated with over 200 images, Arthur Credland takes the reader on a unique pictorial history of Hull's fishing industry and its community; from the role of the trawlers during the two world wars to the amalgamations of the 1960s and '70s, the infamous Cod Wars and the massive reduction of the fleet after 1975. In October 2001 the new £4.5 million Hull fish market, 'Fishgate' opened, starting a new chapter in Hull's fishing heritage.

0-7524-2813-6

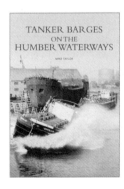

The Wilson Line

ARTHUR G. CREDLAND

Founded in the early years of the nineteenth century, the Wilson Line became the largest privately owned steamship fleet in the world. Based in Hull, its main trade was to and from Scandinavia and the Baltic States although the Wilson Line also carried cargoes to the USA, the Mediterranean and India. Emigrants were an important part of the company's business, with large numbers of Norwegians, Swedes and Jewish refugees of the Tsarist pogroms being brought to Hull, transported overland to Liverpool and shipped to America.

0-7524-1728-2

Tanker Barges on the Humber Waterways

MIKE TAYLOR

This detailed book provides a history of the tanker barges that have moved liquid cargoes on the Humber's inland waterways from the early twentieth century to the present day and is a companion volume to *Tugs and Towing Barges on the Humber Waterways*. Mike Taylor — an avid canal historian — relates the story of the Humber tankers with a wide selection of illustrations interspersed with recollections of men who worked on the waterways.

0-7524-3921-9